Take a Chance

RISKS TO GROW BY

A WORKBOOK FOR A MORE FULFILLING LIFE

JOSEPH ILARDO, PH.D. &

CAROLE R. ROTHMAN, PH.D.

MJF BOOKS
NEW YORK

Publisher's Note: This publication is designed to provide accurate and authoritative information in regard to the subject matter covered. It is sold with the understanding that the publisher is not engaged in rendering psychological, financial, legal, or other professional services. If expert assistance or counseling is needed, the services of a competent professional should be sought.

Author's Note: This book draws on case material, including the experiences of individuals with whom we've worked as teachers and therapists. However, all the names and identifying details have been changed to safeguard privacy. In a few cases, we have created composites to achieve the same end.

Published by MJF Books
Fine Communications
322 Eighth Avenue
New York, NY 10001

Take A Chance
LC Control Number 2002110993
ISBN 1-56731-566-6

Contents

Take a Chance

1

Why Do You Need To Take Risks?

Think back for a minute. What's the biggest risk you ever took? Okay. Now ask yourself: What risk do you most regret *not* having taken?

The answers to those questions very likely summarize your greatest joy and excitement — and your biggest regret. Keep them in mind; for your own experience will serve as a point of reference in the course of the psychological journey you're about to begin.

What's a Risk?

The dictionary defines the word risk as "exposure to the chance of injury or loss; a hazardous or dangerous chance."

Viewed from this broad perspective, there are many, many kinds of risks. Some are unavoidable. Just driving your car to work is a risk. If you live in a typical city, just breathing the air is risky.

These are passive, everyday risks. They don't enrich your life in any significant way. They merely go with the landscape of modern life. They are *not* the focus of this book.

Other risks are deliberate, but they don't really contribute to your growth as a person. The decision to undergo elective surgery is an example of such a risk. So is engaging in physically dangerous sports, such as skydiving and hang gliding.

This book is about one particular type of deliberate risk, the kind that shapes you as a person and gives direction to your life. Each time you take risks of this sort, you are, in effect, creating yourself. You are saying, "This is what I choose; this is who I am."

You take this kind of risk when you commit yourself to another person, invest time and money in developing a talent, or reveal your true feelings for the first time.

Such choices are almost always felt to be risky, because they're accompanied by three feelings: uncertainty (you cannot know the outcome in advance), anxiety (you fear the unknown), and guilt (you must leave behind what you have known and been).

For example, suppose you decide to move across the country, either to go to school or to start a new job. You feel uncertain because you can't predict how your life will change as a result of the move. You feel anxious because you're facing the unknown. And you feel guilty because in choosing to move ahead you're leaving others behind.

These risks also frequently trigger mixed feelings of exhilaration and fear. Think back, for a moment, to the day you learned to ride a two-wheeler. Remember the moment when you looked back and found that no one was holding the seat? You were balancing by yourself! The excitement and fear you felt then are emblematic of the way you feel when you take self-defining risks.

It would be wrong to get the impression that all self-defining risks are monumental in scope. Many may seem rather trivial in themselves, but their significance is far-reaching.

An example is confronting a friend with whom you're angry. Perhaps he has taken you for granted or hurt your feelings in some other way. Rather than say nothing, you decide to let him know exactly how you feel.

Such "trivial" risks hardly seem life-shaping. Yet taking them — or avoiding them — makes you into who you are.

One last point. There's a popular misconception that all significant psychological risks involve movement, change, and excitement. This is true of some — such as getting married, getting a divorce, leaving a job, and going back to school. But others, although less dramatic, are equally significant. You take this low-key kind of risk when you make a commitment to remain loyal to someone when it would be easy not to, and when you resist the urge to do the popular or easy thing.

Are You a Risk-Taker?

To get a quick fix on yourself as a risk-taker, answer the following questions:

Quick Risk Inventory

Yes	No	
X	___	1. Do you have endless debates with yourself every time you have to make a decision — and sometimes wind up making no decision at all?
X	___	2. Do you accept poor service in a restaurant rather than speak up?
X	___	3. Do you have a hard time making emotional commitments to others?
X	___	4. Do you find excuses to stop yourself from getting a better job, learning new skills, or taking advantage of similar opportunities for self-improvement?
X	___	5. Does your fear of the disapproval of others keep you from doing things you want to do?

Any "yes" response indicates that you may shrink from taking significant risks. By habit, you tend to play it safe.

One telltale sign that you are avoiding risks is this: you probably feel frustrated, unhappy, and resentful of the people and circumstances that seem to "hold you back." You may sense that your potential is unrealized; your life may seem flat and uninteresting. You may settle for less than you should, then justify your decision.

Kinds of Risks

There are three kinds of deliberate risks that lead to the expansion of your identity: *self-improvement risks*, *commitment risks*, and *self-disclosure risks*. All three involve a conscious, deliberate choice to put yourself on the line, knowing that there are no guarantees.

There are crucial differences between these three types of risks.

Self-Improvement Risks

You take self-improvement risks in hope of enriching your life in some way. You may take a risk to get ahead, to learn something new, to emerge from the sidelines and into the spotlight. These are the risks that enable you to bridge the gap between what you are and what you can be — to make your dreams become reality. Often, not taking such risks can spawn bitter regrets.

Some self-improvement risks hold the possibility of personal failure. It's often this fear of failure that stops people from taking them.

Asked to describe the single most important risk she wished she had taken, a student wrote:

> The risk I wish I had taken and never did has turned into a bitter regret. I had the opportunity to show my artwork to an art gallery, and possibly win an apprenticeship, but I couldn't work up the nerve. I didn't think my work was good enough. As I relay this event to you I can't help but see that the risks I have regrets over are the ones that might have propelled me forward in life, either economically or emotionally. I guess I have to come to terms with my fears about putting my potential on the line: the biggest fear is that I'm just not good enough. Always keeping that potential a secret has been a way to avoid coming to terms with both my talent *and* my limitations.

Other self-improvement risks may not expose you to the dangers of failure or rejection to quite the same degree. But they may require significant personal sacrifice before you can realize long-term benefits.

The sacrifice can be financial, as might be required when starting your own business or attending special classes to improve your skills at work.

Such risks may also require the sacrifice of changing your routine or giving up what's familiar to you. When you take them, you sacrifice predictability and familiarity for the possibility of growth. Examples range from the relatively trivial (trying an unfamiliar food) to the substantive (living abroad for six months).

Commitment Risks

The popular view of commitment is succinctly expressed in a poster that made the rounds in therapists' offices some years ago. On a brightly colored, psychedelic background, a simple statement is written unevenly, in thick black letters: "In commitment you dash the hopes of a thousand potential selves."

The message could not be farther from the truth. In reality, you define yourself by the commitments you make. If you avoid making commitments, you all but guarantee that your emotional growth will be stunted.

There are two types of commitment risks. With one type, you commit yourself to a person or a relationship. These are the risks you take when you fall in love.

With the other type, you commit yourself to a value, whether it's expressed in a cause, a career, or even a set of criteria you apply before investing in common stocks.

The experience of another individual illustrates what it means to commit yourself to a value. Responding to a question about the biggest risk he'd ever taken, he explained that he'd recently begun working in the human services field because he believed in the importance of the work. "My biggest risk," he wrote, "was leaving a well-paying, secure job, where I had ten years seniority, to work in a field that pays half the money, is new for me, and takes a lot more out of me emotionally then my last job did."

Self-Disclosure Risks

When you open up to others and reveal who you really are, how you feel, and what you want or need, you're taking the risk of self-disclosure.

You take these risks when you confront others with whom you're angry.

Sometimes you risk self-disclosure in the course of working with others, when you must frankly admit that you don't understand something or have failed to perform a task properly because you're confused.

At other times, you may take a self-disclosure risk when you tell someone how you really feel about him or her. One person observed:

> It's difficult for me to express my feelings and make myself vulnerable to ridicule or rejection. I'm more comfortable putting up a front. I would say the biggest risk I've taken, and probably will continue to take, is opening up to people and telling them how much I care for and love them. The expression of positive emotions may not seem risky; but my sense of vulnerability, coupled with my fear of rejection, has always made this very hard for me.

Any communication risk falls into the self-disclosure category. You can't be assertive without taking risks of self-disclosure.

The triangle diagram on the next page shows how the three kinds of risks all contribute to your identity.

Risk-Taking and Security

One of the paradoxes of life is that genuine security requires risk-taking. To understand why, you need to recognize the difference between two kinds of security: *static* and *dynamic*.

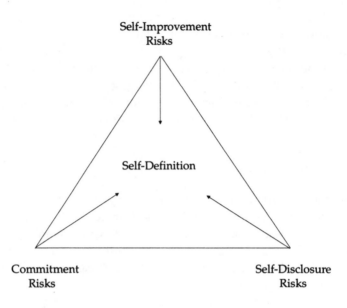

Self-Improvement
Risks

Self-Definition

Commitment
Risks

Self-Disclosure
Risks

Static security implies the absense of change. People who crave static security are likely to say such things as:

- "I can't quit my job because I may never get another."

- "I'd better not break up with him (or her); a dull relationship is better than none at all."

- "Yes, I'd like to say what I'm really thinking, but I don't want to rock the boat."

The person who is "secure" in this sense is likely to be frightened, closed, rigid, and unchanging. Under stress, he or she has trouble coping.

It's a fact that

- Thousands of businesses fail each year because their managers are too inflexible — too committed to static security — to adjust to changes in the marketplace.

- Relationships fall apart because the partners fail to permit change or growth.

- Civilizations have crumbled under the weight of traditions that made it impossible for them to adapt to a changing world.

By contrast, dynamic security implies openness, fluidity, and growth. It's always in the making. It's never quite achieved because it's always unfolding. Viewed this way, dynamic security is like life itself.

Genuinely secure people are risk-takers. They are able to continually risk their sense of security, confident that they can establish a deeper and more satisfying sense of it by opening themselves up.

Here's an example. Ellen is a twenty-three-year-old unmarried secretary. She took her current job when she was a junior in college; that was the year when her parents got a divorce and Ellen felt too upset about it to continue in school. She likes her work and is good at it, but has the strong feeling that she could be doing more with her life. Encouraged by a good friend, Ellen begins thinking seriously about returning to college and finishing her degree in psychology. She starts looking into schools nearby. After some searching, she comes up with one that has a full-time program especially geared to women who are returning to school after an absence of several years. The only drawback is that the program tends to accept women with better academic records than Ellen's. Although she is not at all certain that she'll be admitted, and she's uneasy at the thought of leaving her job and going back to school, Ellen plunges ahead. She completes the application, arranges for the necessary transcripts and letters of recommendation, and waits. When the acceptance finally comes — along with an offer of financial aid — Ellen is at once ecstatic and terrified. She quits her job and starts getting ready for the school year.

Ellen took risks not only when she applied to college, but when she left her job to accept the offer of admission. She was willing to give up the static security of her job to find deeper, more dynamic security on the track of a new career.

The same challenge faces you: to fulfill your potential, you must sacrifice security and take risks.

Like it or not, you can't avoid risk-taking. Many everyday risks — such as breathing polluted air or driving on the freeway — contribute nothing to your development as a person. Neither do a good many deliberate risks that only involve physical dangers. But three particular types of deliberate risks — self-improvement risks, commitment risks, and self-disclosure risks — can help you become more completely yourself.

In the next few chapters, you'll identify the risks you tend to take and the risks you tend to avoid. After that, you'll find out why and learn what to do about it.

2

Taking Stock of Yourself
as a Risk-Taker

On April 4, 1968 Memphis, Tennessee was braced for a protest demonstration. Martin Luther King, Jr. had arrived the day before to lead a peaceful march in support of striking sanitation workers. A week earlier, he'd led a similar march that ended in mayhem and looting. King abhorred violence. He deeply regretted what had happened and was determined that this day's demonstration would not be a repeat of the week before.

The march never took place. On the morning of the 4th, standing on the balcony of his motel room, King was assassinated.

Reverend King had lived life "on the edge" ever since leaving his conventional ministry in Birmingham, Alabama in 1955 to commit himself to righting the wrongs suffered by African-Americans. From that time on, risk and danger were his constant companions. Some of the risks he ran were emotional. He had left a traditional ministry to live the life of an activist, uncertain of the benefits his efforts would yield. His risks were also physical and intensely personal. His house was bombed on February 30, 1956. He was stabbed on September 20, 1958. As the leader of sit-ins and marches all over the South he faced hostile citizens and angry police armed with fire hoses, guard dogs, and loaded weapons. He was arrested, jailed, and "roughed up" many times.

Despite his keen awareness of the dangers he faced, King never wavered. His choices, a source of personal meaning and purpose, fueled his willingness to take extraordinary risks; he moved mountains. Although members of the African-American community were the primary baneficiaries of King's dedication, every American was enriched by it. His courage changed America, and the world, forever. Little wonder that on December 10, 1964 King was awarded the Nobel Peace Prize. Not surprisingly, he applied the entire award—$54,000—to his mission.

Ironically, even though King's birthday is now a national holiday, many of his generation considered him un-American—a trouble-maker of questionable loyalty. Yet, as a citizen of a nation founded and settled by pioneers willing to face unknown dangers and uncertainties, King continued a long-standing tradition of taking chances to pursue a dream. His spiritual companions include American icons such as Lewis and Clark. Abraham Lincoln, and John Glen.

The U. S. has long been regarded as "the land of the free and the home of the brave", and we look up to those willing to take chances. Unfortunately, this admiration for risk-takers extends even to those whose risks are not constructive or even socially sanctioned. Astronauts, entrepreneurs, and social reformers—whose risks are worthy—are indiscriminately linked with other risk-takers, such as daredevils and outlaw heroes. Americans often fail to distinguish between risks that promote personal growth and those that have no effect on it whatsoever.

Our fascination with risk-taking blinds us to a crucial truth: from the point of view of psychological growth, not all risks are created equal. In fact, there are enormous differences between them.

When you take stock of yourself as a risk-taker, the question you must answer is not simply, "Am I taking enough risks?" (After all, it's possible to take countless risks of the wrong sort and not benefit at all!) Rather, the question is, "Am I taking enough risks of the right kind — the kind that promote my growth as a person?"

These questions can only be answered when you know the difference between growth-producing risks and nonproductive ones. In this chapter you'll learn to make that distinction. You'll get help in discovering whether you are wasting your time, energy, and effort on acts of daring that may feel significant but yield no psychological benefits. Knowing the distinction will also help you focus your energy and efforts on risks that are *worth* taking.

In the first part of the chapter, you'll learn about the many characteristics shared both by empty risks and growth-producing ones. Next, you'll discover the hallmarks of non-productive risks: there are several keys that can help you expose them for what they are. Finally, you'll learn the essential features of psychological risks and the distinguishing characteristics of the three types discussed in the previous chapter: self-improvement risks, commitment risks, and self-disclosure risks.

Once you have this information in mind, you'll be in a position to begin targeting those psychological risks you need to begin taking more frequently. In the next chapter, you'll formulate your Personal Risk Profile and your Personal Risk Agenda.

Similarities Between Psychological and Empty Risks

Much confusion is created by the fact that psychological risks and empty ones have a lot in common. There are seven similarities between them:

1. All risk-taking involves a choice. The sky diver who steps out of an airplane at 3,000 feet chooses to do so no less than an alcoholic who makes the decision to attend a meeting of Alcoholics Anonymous (A.A.) for the first time. (The sky diver's risk is an empty one, the alcoholic's isn't.)

2. All risk-taking requires an investment of some sort, whether of time, money, energy, or something else. The sky diver has certainly spent time learning to enjoy his sport. He's paid for lessons. He's memorized procedures, practiced them, and prepared himself for his jump. In these ways, his investment parallels that of the alcoholic, who has gathered information and likely gone through a long series of emotional battles before convincing himself of the need to arrive at the meeting site.

3. All risk-taking can fail. Regardless of the type of risk, success is not guaranteed. There is always the possibility of a "shortfall," a failure of nerves, a devastating loss. The sky diver's chute may fail to deploy. An error in technique might cause an injury or even death. Similarly, the alcoholic might not be able to stop drinking.

4. All risk-taking requires that the risker put himself on the line in some way (for example, financially, physically, or emotionally). In the end, whatever preparations have been made, and whatever excuses might be offered, it is the risk-taker alone who is responsible for the success of his or her efforts. The sky diver either jumps properly and executes a safe landing or suffers the consequences. Similarly, alcoholics — tempted as they might be to place responsibility for their success or failure on the past, their family, their life situation — know that it's they and they alone who must stop drinking. Success or failure rests entirely on the individual involved.

5. All risk-taking is accompanied by feelings of stretching oneself, rising to meet a challenge. The willingness to do this, to leave behind the safety and security of the familiar, is what distinguishes the risk-taker from other people. It's far safer and more comfortable not to risk, not to change, than to venture into the frightening realm of the uncertain. The sky diver defies the fear that keeps some of us on the ground (and most of us safely inside any airplane that carries us aloft!). The alcoholic takes the risk of abandoning an entire lifestyle, changing his friends, perhaps even leaving his dysfunctional family when he makes the decision to dry out.

6. All risk-taking carries important psychic rewards. Feelings of pride and accomplishment accompany all risk-taking. Riskers typically discover new power, strength, and potential within themselves. For many riskers, the feeling is almost a rebirth. Surviving a jump from a plane is similar to being given a new lease on life. Beating an addiction is akin to reclaiming your existence. The "high" that results from such an achievement, regardless of the nature of the risk taken, is an experience all risk-takers share.

7. Virtually all risk-taking sparks feelings of excitement, novelty, movement, and change. This is especially true of psychologically nonproductive risks, and is often true of psychologically productive ones. The experience of jumping out of an airplane can hardly be routine, even for the most experienced sky diver. It carries the excitement, novelty, and element of danger that accounts for much of its appeal. The same can be said for many of the feelings experienced by alcoholics attending their first AA meeting.

These seven important similarities between nonproductive risks and true psychological ones show how easy it is to confuse the two. And yet there are crucial differences between them.

Differences Between Nonproductive and Psychological Risks

What are the characteristics of "empty" risks — those that spark all the excitement of chance-taking but fail to contribute to your psychological maturation?

Characteristics of Nonproductive Risks

Empty risks are set apart from psychological ones by five factors:

1. The source of your motivation

2. The payoff promised

3. The ultimately unsatisfying nature of the risks

4. The illusion they create

5. The potential for loss they carry

1. Empty risks are almost always the product of boredom, restlessness, a lack of fulfillment, or a need to prove yourself. They are taken to fill a void, to introduce meaning and significance into the risk-taker's existence.

The 1955 movie classic, *Rebel without a Cause*, contains a scene that beautifully captures the essence of empty risk-taking. At night, on a high bluff along the California coast, a group of teens has gathered to witness a game of "chicken." Two rival youths are to drive cars straight toward land's end. Theirs is to be a battle of wits, for the one to jump from the car first is the "chicken" and the loser.

The cars line up side by side 100 yards from the edge of the bluff. On signal, the deadly game begins. Tires squeal as the two cars lurch forward and strain to gain speed. Neither driver shows any sign of slowing down or jumping from the car. At the last possible instant, each makes his move. One survives. The other, however, becomes trapped; his car flies over the edge of the bluff, carrying him with it. The survivor joins his fellows as they stand staring at the wreck below. He asks where his opponent is, and learns only then that his rival has been carried to his death. There is a long period of silence. In fear the group disperses.

Despite the horror of the accident, the viewer is left with the distinct impression that incidents like this will occur again. For the game of chicken was born out of boredom and a need to prove oneself. The tragedy of the death is heightened by the absurdity of the motivation behind the contest.

Empty risk-taking is sparked by a desire to overcome a feeling of emptiness by manufacturing excitement, danger, a false sense of being alive by living life "on the edge."

2. Empty risks are taken for thrills. Typically, the excitement itself is the payoff. Like the compulsive gambler, the person who risks for the sake of risking is hooked on the experience of chance-taking itself. The point is not any tangible payoff, although sometimes there is one. Rather, the point is the surge of excitement that accompanies the risking.

3. Empty risks must be repeated and outdone. To achieve the same "high," risk-takers must push themselves further each time. Hang gliders must try longer and more challenging flights. Gamblers must raise the stakes. Rock climbers must scale more treacherous cliffs. The spiral proceeds ever upward. That's why, as Ralph Keyes observes in his book, *Chancing It*, many daredevils' lives end tragically: the one final stunt proves to be too much.

4. Empty risks are almost always symbolic gestures that create the illusion of movement, change, and growth; but they are without substance. Daredevil stunts may *seem* to carry meaning. They may even symbolize the human need to bridge the gap between what we are and what we can be. However, beyond their excitement and danger, they are devoid of substance.

5. Empty risks typically require stakes that are enormously high. Misguided risk-takers believe that the importance of a risk is tied to the size of the loss that's hazarded. They may jeopardize their career, marriage, reputation, or savings — all in an attempt to convince themselves that they're taking a "real" or substantive risk.

Before turning to the characteristics of true psychological risks, take a moment to answer the following questions:

Your Risk-Taking Habits

Yes	Some-times	No	
___	X	___	1. Do you take risks out of boredom, restlessness, a lack of fulfillment in your life, to fill a void and introduce meaning or significance?
___	___	X	2. Do you take risks for the thrills involved? (Is the excitement itself a key payoff in your risk-taking?)
___	___	X	3. Do you find that your risks must be outdone for you to experience the "high" that accompanied your first success?
___	X	___	4. Do your risks create the illusion of movement, change, and growth, but leave you essentially unchanged?
___	___	X	5. Do your risks require that you place life and limb on the line, or jeopardize other important aspects of your existence, without a correspondingly significant potential reward?

If you answered "yes" or "sometimes" to more than two questions, there's a real danger that you're hooked on empty risks. You need to rethink your views on risking, to take chances that are more productive and constructive. Read on for further guidelines.

Characteristics of Growth-Producing Risks

Four key features distinguish growth-producing risks from empty ones:

1. Their effect on your identity or personality.

2. Their effect on your sense of meaning, purpose, and focus in life.

3. Their effect on your development and psychological maturation.

4. Their occasionally nonexciting (and typically nonphysical) nature.

1. Psychological risks affect both your identity and your personality. When you take them, you give shape and direction to your life: they're a statement of choice and responsibility. For example, when you choose to form a long-term tie with another person, you play an active part in creating yourself and your future. In addition, when you make such a choice, you assume responsibility for the life you fashion.

This is in sharp contrast to the relatively trivial impact of psychologically empty risks. A hang glider or motorcycle stunt rider can hardly be said to give shape or direction to his life as a result of the risks he takes. Though he experiences high levels of excitement, and may live through great danger, his identity and personality remain essentially unchanged.

2. Psychological risks exert a significant influence on your sense of purpose, meaning, and focus in life. This influence can range from important to profound. For example, returning to school as an adult provides a focus for your energies, and channels your intelligence and creativity in one direction for a considerable length of time.

Your sense of meaning and purpose is even more profoundly affected when you commit yourself to a set of values or a cause. The life of Rev. Martin Luther King, Jr. was the product of such a commitment. Deciding to tutor inner-city children, visit someone in a convalescent home, or participate in a neighborhood recycling project can involve a similar change and commitment on a smaller scale.

Frivolous and empty risks, no matter how involving they may be, exert no such influence on your sense of purpose, meaning, and focus.

3. Psychological risks promote your emotional development. They move you along toward higher levels of psychological maturation.

With every psychological risk you take, you are choosing personal growth over stagnation. For example, signing a petition opposing an unjust or discriminatory promotion policy in your place of employment does more than put you "on record" as feeling a certain way. The action, taken with awareness, promotes your psychological maturity by defining you (to yourself as well as others) as a person of courage and character. Just writing your name is a relatively trivial action; but in this context it has profound implications for the growth and development of your identity as a person.

On the other hand, a failure to take a necessary risk may result in your being "stuck" psychologically. It may even result in a movement backwards. The child who is afraid to go to school is a source of concern to parents, because he or she can only move ahead by breaking the ties to mother and venturing into unfamiliar territory. The wife who denies her intelligence and stifles her opinions to keep peace at home loses herself in her marriage. She fails to develop as a person. The corporate executive who remains silent while his company pollutes the environment fails his potential in the same way. Each time you shrink back from taking such a risk, you move one step backwards in your evolution as a fully realized individual.

4. **Although some psychological risks are exciting and even dangerous, not all of them are.** Commitment to a value may be mortally dangerous. Martin Luther King, Jr. died for what he believed in. So did Mahatma Ghandi. Mother Theresa risked her life every day. There are countless examples of people who have suffered death, imprisonment, and torture for what they believed in: Raoul Wallenberg, Benito Aquino, and Anwar Sadat are just a few names that come to mind.

Other psychological risks have dangers and excitement on a more modest scale — marrying or divorcing, for example. But many psychological risks are neither exciting nor dramatic. The choice to remain faithful to your spouse when it would be easy not to is one such example. The choice to continue with a job that helps people, despite offers of more exciting or more lucrative work, is equally risky.

Challenging yourself is often a key to personal growth and development. For example, the aspiring dancer knows she must take increasingly greater risks if she is to progress. Similarly, the skier knows he must master more challenging slopes to develop his skills fully. This is also true for the businessperson who knows she must take on more challenging assignments, and for the pianist who knows he must master increasingly challenging pieces. The danger and excitement inherent in such risk-taking is directly proportional to the personal development produced by challenging yourself. The risks aren't empty, because the objective is more than a "high." Rather, the goal is to move a step closer to what you're capable of becoming.

Distinctions Between the Different Types of Psychological Risks

All risks are similar in at least seven ways, and there are crucial differences between empty risks and psychological ones. It's important to learn to distinguish between the different types of psychological risks as well.

Self-improvement risks, commitment risks, and self-disclosure risks can be distinguished from one another using four criteria:

1. Each type of risk has its own set of potential adverse outcomes; sometimes these differ in nature, sometimes in degree.

2. Each type of risk requires that you make unique sacrifices, incur certain costs, or "invest" in certain ways.

3. Each type of risk is accompanied by a certain mix of feelings, sometimes differing in kind and sometimes in degree.

4. Each type of risk, when successful, produces specific results or effects — some of these results are external, others are internal.

The following summaries highlight these differences.

Self-Improvement Risks

What they are: Any actions taken to improve or develop yourself as a person, to overcome a problem or deficit, to enhance your life, or to broaden your range of skills or experience.

Examples: Returning to school as an adult; mastering a skill (learning an instrument or a sport, creating art, or deepening your appreciation of your world); trying out for a part in a play or orchestra; entering therapy; attending an AA meeting or other self-help group; volunteering for a challenging assignment on the job or in your community; trying out for a competitive scholarship or award.

Adverse consequences: You may fail at what you try to do. What you achieve may fall short of what you hoped to achieve. There may be little or no payoff for the effort you expend. You may lose status. You may be mocked or teased by others. Things may become worse than they were prior to taking the risk.

Costs you may incur, sacrifices you must make: Time, energy, effort, money. You may put your pride and/or reputation on the line. You may jeopardize important relationships.

Accompanying feelings: Anxiety about moving beyond your "comfort zone." Excitement about changing and novelty. Self-doubt ("Can I do the job? Am I up to the task?"). Fear of how others may react if you succeed or fail. If your risk requires that you spend money on yourself, you may worry about whether you're worth the investment.

Net results when successful: You develop your talents, deepen your understanding. You may improve your social standing, income level, and so on. You may move into the limelight, enjoy new satisfactions, experience new feelings and places. New worlds may open up to you, new demands may be made on you. You may discover new strength, new potential, new possibilities within yourself. You feel good about yourself; you may create works of art or scholarship worthy of note. Your self-esteem is improved, along with your sense of personal serenity. You are glad to be alive.

Commitment Risks

What they are: Any actions that involve putting yourself on the line on behalf of a higher cause or value.

Examples: Contribute to a cause, charity, political campaign. Volunteer to work for a cause, charity, candidate. Join a movement or organization. Marry or establish a monogamous tie. Have or adopt a child. Lobby for change, write to your Senator, lead a protest movement.

Adverse consequences: Rejection, disapproval; loss of status, jobs, friends. In extreme cases, imprisonment, death; frustration or disappointment if you've committed yourself to a disappointing person or cause.

Costs you may incur, sacrifices you must make: Time, energy, effort, money. You put your pride and/or reputation on the line. You make an emotional investment. You may sacrifice your physical health or security. You may jeopardize important relationships.

Accompanying feelings: Anxiety about putting yourself on the line emotionally, financially, physically, or in other ways. Helplessness at being unable to know or control the outcome of your action. Panic or resignation when you realize that there's no going back (some choices can't be reversed). Disappointment or resignation as you accept or affirm your own limitations. Guilt about disappointing others who wish you'd made different choices.

Net result when successful: Stronger sense of identity ("This is who I am.") Stronger sense of independence. You discover new strength, new potential, new power within yourself. You simultaneously discover and express your courage. You are seen as a person with convictions. You experience an increased sense of purpose, meaning in your life. Your life has a new focus. You exert influence in righting a wrong, promoting something you believe in, defeating apathy or evil.

Self-Disclosure Risks

What they are: Any actions that result in others knowing your wants, likes, feelings, preferences, goals, etc.

Examples: Assertive behavior, including expressing your feelings when you're attracted to someone, confronting someone with whom you're upset, making your wants known without apologizing; openly supporting an unpopular cause; revealing something about you others might not be aware of ("I'm gay," "I'm an alcoholic," etc.); questioning or challenging a standing policy or an authority (such as nuns who protested when the Pope visited the United States); starting a conversation with a stranger; expressing your interest in someone; asking someone out on a date.

Adverse consequences: Rejection (your overtures may be rejected); disapproval. You may be seen as pushy, forward, or disrespectful. You may not get what you want. You may lose friends, your job (if you challenge your boss or lead a strike). You may be laughed at. In extreme cases, you may be imprisoned or even lose your life.

Costs you may incur, sacrifices you must make: You must declare yourself — let your feelings, wants, views, and preferences be known either in person or some other way (such as a letter to the editor). Getting your views out may require time, effort, energy, money, and other kinds of personal sacrifices. You may risk wounding your pride or suffer a loss of status.

Accompanying feelings: Fear about being exposed and vulnerable. Anxiety about putting yourself on the line emotionally or in other ways. Uncertainty about how others will react and frustration about your inability to control their reactions. Guilt about disappointing others whose image of you may be shattered. Pride in finding the emotional resources within yourself to take this risk. Excitement about the possibility of succeeding.

Net results when successful: Increased confidence that comes from letting others know who you really are, what you want, how you feel. People take you seriously and may respect you more. You feel more in control of your life. You like and respect yourself more. You may get what you want more often. You may wind up doing fewer things you don't want to do. People see you as "up front" and honest. You discover new personal strength, possibilities, and potentials. You amaze yourself with what you have achieved.

In the next chapter, you will assess your personal risk profile and formulate your personal risk agenda. Both of these tools will help guide you in your relationship to risk-taking and psychological growth.

Further Reading

Keyes, R. (1985) *Chancing It*. Boston: Little, Brown and Co.

3

What Kinds of Risks
Do You Need To Take?

How often do you take psychological risks? Of the three types (self-improvement, commitment, self-disclosure), which do you tend to take most often? Are there risks you should be taking but aren't? Are there others you need not — or should not — continue taking?

In this chapter you'll answer these questions. Using what you've already learned about risk-taking, plus your personal risk profile inventory score, you'll formulate a personal risk profile and agenda for change.

Part One: Your Personal Risk Profile

How To Complete the Inventory

The inventory you will soon complete contains 30 statements. You will be asked to indicate how strongly you agree or disagree with each one.

Some of the statements simply express a point of view (for example, "I get no joy out of risking my life for fun, but I enjoy the less dramatic risks of loving others and committing myself to them."). When you respond to such statements, your personal opinion is all that's needed. Write your score in the appropriate column to reflect how strongly you agree or disagree with that point of view (the scores are listed above each response).

Other inventory items require that you say what you are like or recall how you have behaved recently (for example, "Within the past few years, I've devoted a lot of time and effort to developing a talent I'd never tried to develop before."). When responding, write your score in the column that best indicates your reaction.

Still other statements require that you say how you would react in a hypothetical situation (for example, "If I were to witness a crime, I would volunteer at a subsequent trial, despite the inconvenience and possible dangers."). When you "somewhat agree" with this kind of statement, you are saying that the behavior described is partly true of you: you would behave as described at least some of the time. When you "mostly disagree," you're saying that the statement is not particularly true of you, or that you would usually not behave as described in the statement. When you "disagree strongly," you're saying that the statement isn't true of you at all. You should only score the "neutral" column when you're absolutely certain that you could not agree or disagree, or when you absolutely cannot predict whether you would behave as described. You can also score the neutral column if, for some reason, the question is completely inapplicable to your life or circumstances.

Regardless of the type of statement you're responding to, try not to score the neutral column too often.

It will take about ten minutes to complete the inventory. Follow these guidelines:

- Be honest. The most useful answers are those that genuinely capture you as you really are.

- Accept the statements at face value, and resist the temptation to discover any hidden meanings behind them.

- When you're asked to respond to a hypothetical situation, respond as though you were confronting the situation at the present time. Avoid responding as you might have several years ago, or as you might several years from now.

- With these instructions in mind, please read each statement and write your score in the column that best reflects your position.

Personal Risk Profile Inventory

	4 Agree strongly	3 Agree somewhat	2 Neutral	1 Mostly disagree	0 Disagree strongly
1. I'm not content to do things half way. When I discover that I have a skill, I work to develop it fully.					
2. If I had the opportunity to participate in a potentially explosive public demonstration in support of some cause I believe in deeply, I would participate, despite the risks involved.					
3. I tend to open up to people quite often, even though I'm not always comfortable when I do.					
4. When I really want to improve myself in some way, I'm willing to invest time and effort to do it.					
5. I get no joy out of risking myself for fun, but I enjoy the less dramatic risks of loving others and committing myself to them.					
6. If I felt taken advantage of by a family member or friend, I would let that person know how I felt.					
7. I am the sort of person who enjoys trying new things and discovering new possibilities within myself, even when doing so costs me a lot.					
8. If I became aware of fraud, corruption, or employee theft in the business where I work, I would report it to my superiors.					
9. When I need a favor from someone close to me, I can almost always ask for it without much discomfort.					

Personal Risk Profile Inventory

page 2

	4 Agree strongly	3 Agree somewhat	2 Neutral	1 Mostly disagree	0 Disagree strongly
10. I resist getting into ruts, and prefer taking a chance on new things, even if I feel uncomfortable doing them.					
11. If I believe in some value or principle (for example, a person's right to privacy), I will put myself on the line to see that the value or principle is upheld.					
12. If I were dissatisfied with a product I purchased, I would return the item and voice my dissatisfaction, even if the retailer from whom I bought it had a "no returns" policy.					
13. If I were given an opportunity to improve my education or develop my skills, I would take it, even at a considerable inconvenience or personal expense.					
14. At one point in my life, I lost friends because I stood up for a principle I believed in.					
15. If I wanted to date someone but I wasn't sure he or she was interested in me, I'd take a chance and ask him or her out anyway.					
16. Within the past few years, I've devoted a lot of time and effort to developing a talent I'd never tried to develop before.					

Personal Risk Profile Inventory

page 3

	4 Agree strongly	3 Agree somewhat	2 Neutral	1 Mostly disagree	0 Disagree strongly
17. If I were to witness a crime, I would volunteer at a subsequent trial, despite the inconvenience and possible dangers.					
18. If I were at a party with friends and someone proposed doing something I objected to (suppose, for example, that the host offered crack cocaine to the guests), I would speak out forcefully against the idea, even though I might be seen as a wet blanket by the other guests.					
19. If I were given a chance to break into a new and exciting career, I would certainly give it my best shot, even if there were no assurances that I would succeed.					
20. Despite all the uncertainties associated with forming close, long-term ties with people outside my family, I have formed and maintained at least a few such ties in my life.					
21. I enjoy starting conversations and making friends with strangers I meet when I travel.					
22. If given the choice between a familiar and secure job and an exciting one that makes new demands on me, I'd try the new job, even if it meant that I'd have to give up some security.					

Personal Risk Profile Inventory

page 4

	4 Agree strongly	3 Agree somewhat	2 Neutral	1 Mostly disagree	0 Disagree strongly
23. If I were with people and someone told an offensive ethnic joke, I would voice my displeasure, even if that meant that others might think me too serious or high-minded.					
24. My friends and family know that I'm not afraid to ask questions in any situation, regardless of whether I may appear foolish to others.					
25. I'm determined to do all I can to live out my dreams, even if that means that I must risk failure to do so.					
26. I can't just sit by and watch while vulnerable people are treated cruelly or unfairly; I feel obligated to try to intervene.					
27. I am quick to state my opinions.					
28. I welcome the opportunity to take on tough assignments at work and in most other contexts.					
29. I feel sorry for people who don't commit themselves to other people and to the values that matter in life.					
30. If I were in line at the supermarket and someone tried to get ahead of me, I'd quickly let him or her know that I was there first.					

Scoring Your Inventory

Begin by looking at the three lists of inventory item numbers on the scoresheet below. On the line next to each inventory item number, write the number of points you scored for that item.

Next, total up the number of points for each column.

Finally, add up your three subtotal scores and place the grand total on the line indicated.

Personal Risk Profile Inventory Scoresheet

List One		List Two		List Three	
Inventory Item Number	Points Earned	Inventory Item Number	Points Earned	Inventory Item Number	Points Earned
1	_____	2	_____	3	_____
4	_____	5	_____	6	_____
7	_____	8	_____	9	_____
10	_____	11	_____	12	_____
13	_____	14	_____	15	_____
16	_____	17	_____	18	_____
19	_____	20	_____	21	_____
22	_____	23	_____	24	_____
25	_____	26	_____	27	_____
28	_____	29	_____	30	_____
Subtotal One	_____	Subtotal Two	_____	Subtotal Three	_____

Grand Total _____

How To Interpret Your Scores

The first score you should interpret is your grand total. This number tells you how strongly you're inclined to take psychological risks or to avoid them. Use the following as a guide:

Grand Total	Meaning

When it comes to taking psychological risks in general,

91-120	you are strongly inclined to take such risks.
61-90	you are moderately inclined to take such risks.
31-60	you tend to avoid such risks.
0-30	you are extremely disinclined to take such risks.

Each subtotal from the risk profile scoresheet corresponds to one of the three types of psychological risks, and gives you a good idea of the extent to which you take that type of risk.

Subtotal	Type of Risk
One	Self-improvement
Two	Commitment
Three	Self-disclosure

Interpret each subtotal score by using the key below for each of the three types of risks.

Subtotal Score	Interpretation
31-40	You are strongly inclined to take such risks.
21-30	You are moderately inclined to take such risks.
11-20	You tend to avoid such risks.
0-10	You are extremely disinclined to take such risks.

Representing Your Profile Graphically

To "see" your personal risk profile, use the blank graph that follows the example. On the extreme left is a vertical axis that reflects the range of subtotal scores from 0 to 40.

Sample Risk Profile

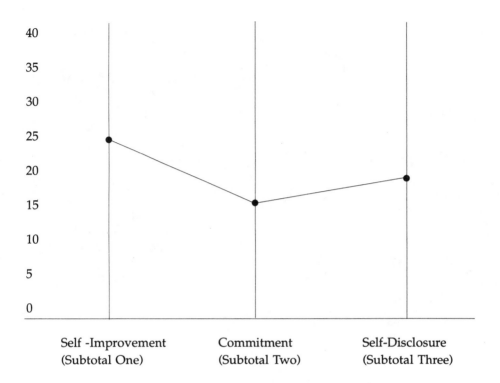

Along the bottom of the graph (the horizontal axis) are the three types of psychological risks. Above each type of risk is a vertical line.

Using the extreme left axis as a guide, record the subtotal score above each type of risk. Record your score on the vertical line by placing a point there corresponding to your numeric subtotal, somewhere between 0 and 40. By connecting the three points you've plotted, you will get a "profile line." (The heights of the points you plot indicate your relative inclination to risk in each way. The lower the point, the less inclined you are to take risks of that type. The higher the point, the more inclined you are to take such risks.)

Interpreting Your Scores

Now that you've completed and scored your inventory and arrived at your Personal Risk Profile, think about what the numbers mean. Are you more or less of a psychological

Your Risk Profile

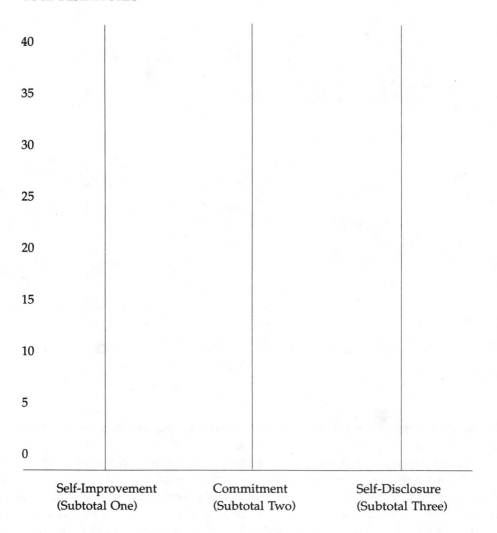

	Self-Improvement	Commitment	Self-Disclosure
40			
35			
30			
25			
20			
15			
10			
5			
0			
	Self-Improvement	Commitment	Self-Disclosure
	(Subtotal One)	(Subtotal Two)	(Subtotal Three)

risk-taker than you imagined? Consider the kinds of risks you take and avoid. Do they reflect what's really important to you?

If your scores are high for all three kinds of psychological risks, read on to sharpen your skills and deepen your understanding.

If you are moderately inclined to risk overall, you should pay special attention to the kinds of risks you tend to avoid. If you feel a need to take more of them, later chapters will help you learn how.

If you avoid risking in most of the situations described, and if you're dissatisfied with that, it's important to understand the reasons for your avoidance. The next few chapters will help you do that. Chapters 4, 5, and 6 will be particularly useful in freeing you to take more risks.

Part Two: Your Personal Risk Agenda

An agenda is a plan, a series of steps to be followed in accomplishing some purpose. A well run business meeting is almost always governed by an agenda. The person who prepares the agenda identifies tasks to be accomplished, sets priorities, and decides the order in which items will be acted upon.

In the same way, your risk-taking should be governed by an agenda. Your Personal Risk Agenda is a product of what you now know about the different kinds of risks and your knowledge about your particular scores on the inventory. An agenda will help direct your risk-taking efforts.

There are really two agendas: a general one that provides a broad view of your status as a risk-taker and can guide your overall risk-taking behavior, and a specific one that helps identify the specific risks you may need to take in light of the particular circumstances of your life.

Formulating Your General Risk Agenda

To formulate your general agenda, answer the questions that follow as best you can. You may not be able to answer all questions as completely and specifically as you'd like. For example, don't expect to be able to completely explain your reluctance to risk. Nevertheless, answer each question as fully as possible. A sample questionnaire with answers follows at the end of this exercise.

General Risk Agenda Worksheet

My Status as a Risk-Taker

Am I taking as many risks as I'd like? Why or why not?

Am I taking the kinds of risks I want to take? Why or why not?

My Risk-Taking Tendencies

Am I taking too many risks of the wrong kind? (In other words, am I risking recklessly and foolishly?)

I may not be risking foolishly — but am I taking the kinds of psychological risks that can make my life more meaningful and satisfying? Am I taking these risks as frequently as I would like?

Do I tend to avoid certain risks or to take them less often than I'd like? Why? How is my life affected by that avoidance?

What priorities for my risk-taking do I want to set? In other words, of the various psychological risks I'm not taking as often as I'd like, which ones are most important to me? Which ones are least important to me? (For help in answering this question, complete the "My Values and Priorities Checklist" on the next page. On the space next to each item listed, write a number that reflects its importance to you. Use this scale: 0 = not important at all, 2 = minimally important, 3 = somewhat important, 4 = quite important, 5 = extremely important.)

My Values and Priorities Checklist

In my life I want

___ a career that's meaningful

___ opportunities to work for important social values

___ a chance to live with complete independence for a time

___ gratifying relationships

___ excitement, change, novelty, and variety in abundance

___ a chance to devote myself to causes that matter to me

___ opportunities to travel and experience different cultures and ways of life

___ status and prestige

___ the peace of mind that comes from knowing myself fully

___ a chance to have a positive impact on my society

___ an opportunity to settle down with one partner and raise a family

___ a chance to acquire enough wealth to live out my fantasies

___ opportunities to learn about my world in great detail

___ respect from others, based on my extensive knowledge of some subject

___ the self-confidence that comes from being able to comfortably handle any interpersonal confrontation

___ an opportunity to shape and lead an organization

___ plenty of chances for quiet contemplation in a setting that's not competitive or high-pressure

___ the self-assurance that comes from being able to speak with poise and force in front of large audiences

___ the opportunity to create beautiful things as an artist, musician, writer, or in some other creative capacity

___ the satisfaction that comes from being comfortable enough with myself to let others know who I really am

Sample Questionnaire With Answers

My Status as a Risk-Taker

Am I taking as many risks as I'd like? Why or why not?

> *I'm not happy with my life. I don't take many chances. My life is pretty dull. My career is going nowhere. We even go to the same place for vacation year after year. I think I'm so afraid of making mistakes, I tend to do things*

*that are familiar to me over and over again without paying much attention
to whether I find them satisfying.*

Am I taking the kinds of risks I want to take? Why or why not?

*I don't take self-fulfillment risks at all. Instead of taking chances on things
that might lead to more joy, I try to hold on to things I know. I'm so
frustrated. Also, I hate it when people are displeased or angry with me. I
hardly ever take self-disclosure risks. I don't confront people when I'm
upset with them. I guess I dread facing their anger. And I'm often obsessed
with not wanting to hurt other people's feelings.*

My Risk-Taking Tendencies

Am I taking too many risks of the wrong kind? (In other words, am I risking recklessly
and foolishly?)

*I'm not really into reckless risk-taking. I don't sky dive or push myself to
the limit doing dangerous stunts. But sometimes I wonder why I get so
reckless in my car. I drive awfully fast. And I get really angry when other
drivers cut me off or do other stupid things. When I do something dangerous to get even (like cutting them off aggressively or slowing way down
without warning), I seem to be acting for reasons I can't figure out. Maybe
that's my way of making up for not taking more important and worthwhile
risks.*

I may not be risking foolishly — but am I taking the kinds of psychological risks that can
make my life more meaningful and satisfying? Am I taking these risks as frequently as I
would like?

*I can't remember the last time I really took a chance that might have made
my life better. The less I take chances that can improve my life, the more
frightened I become when I think about doing it.*

Do I tend to avoid certain risks or to take them less often than I'd like? Why? How is my
life affected by that avoidance?

*The risks I avoid are mainly those that can help me live better and feel
better about myself. I do take some risks that benefit others. For example,
I did volunteer in the soup kitchen last Thanksgiving. But there are two
kinds of risks I consistently avoid. I almost always step aside when I have
a chance to take on a challenging assignment at work. I guess I doubt my
ability to pull it off. So I step aside and let others meet the challenge —*

reap the rewards. The other kinds are the ones that would put me out on a limb. I don't confront others. I don't let people know how I feel or what I need. My boss probably has no idea that I'm frustrated at work. He'd have to be a mind-reader to know it, because I'm just not willing to risk telling him.

What priorities for my risk-taking do I want to set? In other words, of the various psychological risks I'm not taking as often as I'd like to, which ones are most important to me? Which ones are least important to me?

If I'm going to turn things around and find more fulfillment in my life, I've got to begin overcoming my fear of failure and my fear of displeasing others. A meaningful and satisfying career is really important to me (priority rating 5). To achieve that, I've got to take more risks on the job. I've got to cultivate friendships and learn from others. I've got to be willing to ask questions and to admit that I don't know everything. I've got to be willing to push myself a bit and take on jobs that stretch me to the limit.

Also, it's unrealistic to expect that others will satisfy my needs if I don't let them know what they are! Gratifying relationships are really important to me (priority rating 4). But I can't expect my relationships to be gratifying if I don't let people know who I really am and how I feel about things.

So, as to the risks I've got to begin taking more often, self-fulfillment and self-disclosure are high on the list. On the other hand, I don't really need to take many more commitment risks. I've already shown that I can commit myself to people and causes.

Your Specific Risk Agenda

The sample questionnaire can help you formulate a general risk agenda. But you'll need to examine your current circumstances closely to create a more specific agenda.

Begin this process by facing your dissatisfactions and the sources of displeasure in your life. Confront the specific problems and "short falls" that bother you. Once you do, you can begin targeting specific risks. The following three examples illustrate what we mean.

Example One

When Barbara's high school classmate died in a drunk driving accident, Barbara decided she could no longer remain on the sidelines in the fight against teen alcohol abuse. She decided to start a chapter of S.A.D.D. (Students Against Driving Drunk) on her high school campus. She knew this might make her unpopular with some of her peers. She also knew it would require the cooperation of both the administration and the student body, which she would have to work hard to secure. The sort of risk she took was a commitment risk.

Example Two

After teaching college for five years, Bernie knew that what he enjoyed most was helping students solve their personal problems. He knew he had a knack for it, since students so often came to him for help. Nevertheless, Bernie knew he lacked the expertise to be as helpful as he wished. He decided to return to graduate school to prepare for a career in mental health. Over the next five years, while continuing to teach college, he attended school, earned an M.S.W., and in the end maintained a dual career as a college professor and a psychiatric social worker. The type of risk he took was a self-fulfillment risk.

Example Three

Robin was the youngest of three sisters. Married, with two teenage children, she worked full time as a travel agent. Although her two sisters lived nearby, responsibility for the care of their elderly, widowed mother fell on Robin's shoulders. She felt taken for granted, and decided to speak with both sisters. The kind of risk she took was a self-disclosure risk.

In all three cases, the circumstances of each individual's life gave rise to dissatisfactions and determined the specific risk he or she had to take.

Starting below, you'll have an opportunity to identify the sources of dissatisfaction in your own life and to begin planning for the specific risks you need to take to feel more satisfied. There's a worksheet provided for doing this, along with a few examples of how to use it. Make several photocopies of the worksheet so that you can explore the issues surrounding more than one risk you'd like to take.

Specific Personal Risk Agenda Worksheet

Dissatisfaction
I feel   *(Identify the dissatisfaction)*

Risk I need to take   *(Describe the risk as specifically as possible)*
to overcome
my dissatisfaction

Type of risk this would be (Self-Fulfillment, Commitment, Self-Disclosure)	*(Identify the type of risk)*
Priority rating (5 = highest, 1 = lowest)	*(Assign a value that reflects the personal importance you assign to this risk)*
People and circumstances that affect my taking of this risk	*(Identify the key variables that have an impact on whether or not you take this risk)*
Fears or other obstacles (including my upbringing and past experiences) that may keep me from taking this risk	*(Describe the impediments as fully as you can)*
Things I need to learn or be able to do before taking this risk	*(Describe the groundwork that you must lay in order to take this risk successfully)*

Here are a few examples of how to use the worksheet:

Example One: Peter
Specific Personal Risk Agenda Worksheet

Dissatisfaction I feel	*My sexual life with my partner is monotonous and less satisfying than I'd like.*
Risk I need to take to overcome my dissatisfaction	*I need to convey my desire for a more varied and satisfying sex life.*
Type of risk this would be (Self-Fulfillment, Commitment, Self-Disclosure)	*Self-disclosure (I must make my feelings and wants known).*

Priority rating (5 = highest, 1 = lowest)	4

People and circumstances that affect my taking of this risk	*I'm concerned that my partner will be hurt or angry if I express myself.*

Fears or other obstacles (including my upbringing and past experiences) that may keep me from taking this risk	*My strict, sexually repressive upbringing makes it hard to talk about sex and makes me feel selfish in asking for more sexual gratification.*

Things I need to learn or be able to do before taking this risk	*I have to work on becoming more comfortable with my sexuality and I have to understand that I'm not responsible for my partner's reactions, whatever they are.*

Example Two: Brenda
Specific Personal Risk Agenda Worksheet

Dissatisfaction I feel	*My current dead-end job is unsatisfying.*

Risk I need to take to overcome my dissatisfaction	*I need to find a more fulfilling job.*

Type of risk this would be (Self-Fulfillment, Commitment, Self-Disclosure)	*Self-fulfillment (I may have to try something unfamiliar in order to make my life more satisfying).*

Priority rating (5 = highest, 1 = lowest)	3

People and circumstances that affect my taking of this risk	*My family depends on my income — or I can't just quit my job without having another lined up. Also, the job market is awful now!*

Fears or other obstacles (including my upbringing and past experiences) that may keep me from taking this risk

My needs for security are going to make it hard to give up a "safe" and familiar position for a new and uncertain one.

Things I need to learn or be able to do before takingthis risk

I need to take stock of my skills, prepare a resume, and sharpen my interview technique.

Example Three: Marla
Specific Personal Risk Agenda Worksheet

Dissatisfaction I feel

I'm not doing enough to help victims of racial prejudice.

Risk I need to take to overcome my dissatisfaction

I need to play a more active role in racial politics and the fight against social injustice.

Type of risk this would be (Self-Fulfillment, Commitment, Self-Disclosure)

Commitment

Priority rating (5 = highest, 1 = lowest)

4

People and circumstances that affect my taking of this risk

My job and family responsibilities limit the amount of time and energy I can put into this work.

Fears or other obstacles (including my upbringing and past experiences) that may keep me from taking this risk

I don't like being seen as a crusader. Friends and associates may find me boring. Aunt Jenny was always raising money for the church — and she became a running joke in the family, someone who just didn't know how to relax and have fun. I'd hate to have my children think of me as an "Aunt Jenny" type of person!

| Things I need to learn or be able to do before taking this risk | *I need to take stock of my talents and decide how I can really be of help. This will mean looking hard at my own feelings about racism and activism — and Aunt Jenny!* |

Your personal risk profile and agenda are both unique. Together, they provide a complete picture of you as a risk-taker.

To use them wisely, it's important to do more than simply acknowledge them. Completing the inventory in this chapter and determining your agenda are only the first steps in a process of personal evolution.

By examining your profile, you'll be able to identify the risks you need to take more often. For example, if your profile shows that you tend to avoid commitment risks, you need to take advantage of every reasonable opportunity to live by principles you believe in. Uncomfortable as you may at first feel, stand up for your convictions.

Similarly, if your profile reveals that you're reluctant to reveal yourself to others, begin disclosing more of yourself — initially in relatively safe situations, and later in riskier ones.

While your profile and agenda will point you in the direction of the risks you need to take, they can't tell you which specific risks count most in your life right now. To identify those, you'll need to examine your current circumstances and set your own priorities.

If you're very unhappy in some aspect of your life, chances are good that that unhappiness can be traced back to your reluctance to take one or another risk. Place that risk at the top of your "hit list." Plan for it — later chapters will show you how — and follow through.

If this all sounds more easily said than done, you're right. If it were all so simple, you'd be risking as often as you'd like in many situations. Something, of course, has been holding you back.

At the root of all reluctance to risk is fear. Just being aware of your profile and agenda won't enable you to make the changes you wish. Nor is it enough to resolve to take the risks you've placed at the top of your hit list. You must also identify the fears that keep you from risking. In the next chapter, you'll have an opportunity to identify those fears. In subsequent chapters, you'll learn specific strategies for overcoming your fears.

Further Reading

Morscher, B., and B. Schindler-Jones. (1982) *Risk-taking for Women*. New York: Everest House Publishers. (*The "Values and Priorities Checklist" was based on a similar checklist in this excellent book.*)

4

Understanding Your Fears

Chances are you avoid taking risks because you're afraid. You may fear failing. You may dread the disapproval of your peers. Perhaps you fear that your actions will be misinterpreted. You may even be afraid of succeeding.

There is nothing bad or unusual about being afraid. In fact, fear can be a personal alarm clock, rousing you to make the necessary preparations for your risk-taking.

But fear can also be debilitating. When it is extreme and irrational, it can keep you from taking risks that are important to your personal and professional life.

When 33-year-old Tracy was in the tenth year of a secure managerial job at a large corporation, one of her fundamental beliefs was shattered. Tracy had been raised to believe that hard work — good work — would inevitably lead to success. A bright woman and an excellent employee, Tracy had loyally devoted nearly a third of her life to the corporation she was part of. During the early years of her career, when colleagues were promoted before her, Tracy remained patient. She was convinced that her turn would come. She rationalized that the others were more experienced than she. As time passed and the same thing kept happening, she told herself that she needed to learn more about company politics. Although she was convinced that hard work alone should be enough to yield rewards, Tracy tried being more political. Believing that she needed new communication skills, she completed an assertiveness training course. Nevertheless, advancement continued to elude her.

In the months preceding her tenth anniversary at the company, not one but two less experienced, less industrious colleagues were promoted above Tracy. The awful truth was unavoidable: she was not going to be promoted at this company. Her self-esteem plummeted. She could feel her self-confidence ebbing away.

Tracy was facing a crisis. To stay with the corporation meant security and a reasonable living, but at a tremendous psychological cost. To leave meant sacrificing security and perhaps accepting lower pay or a period of unemployment. The advantage of leaving would be getting a fresh start and an opportunity to see whether she would be able to grow professionally somewhere else.

Among the many feelings Tracy experienced when she reached the crossroads were two kinds of fear. The first was tied to the situation she found herself in. Should she risk leaving the secure job she knew so well? Would her experience at another company be any different?

The second kind of fear was internal. Perhaps she didn't have what it took to make it in the business world. Was her work as good as she thought? Did she lack some skill or attitude that was crucial to success? How would she cope if she failed to win a promotion at yet another company?

Despite these misgivings, Tracy conquered her fears and left her position. She accepted a job with a smaller, rapidly growing firm. Her new position demanded more work and paid less. But it offered her an opportunity to advance. Within months, Tracy's hard work and competence were recognized. She was promoted. Before long, she was promoted again. In less than eighteen months, she was earning more than she had at her previous job. Her responsibilities were greater. The satisfactions she had long awaited were finally hers. "My only regret," she observed, "was that I waited so long to leave."

As Tracy's experience shows, fear — both situational and internal — is an essential component in all risking. Moreover, whether or not your fear is well-founded, acknowledging it is an essential first step in taking important psychological risks. Unless you acknowledge your fear, you'll be powerless to do anything about it. For example, you can't begin to overcome self-doubt unless you first admit it to yourself. Similarly, if your fear is situational and based on a realistic appraisal of some risk of danger, you must look it in the eye before you will be able to respond appropriately.

How This Book Can Help

Don't expect your fear to disappear entirely if you do what this book recommends. You will always be frightened when you take risks. In fact, in *Chancing It*, Ralph Keyes says that no action can be described as "risky" if it fails to generate at least a little fear. Only in fiction are there fearless heroes. Real heroes feel fear, do what they can to overcome it, and proceed.

If you can't expect to rid yourself of fear by reading the next few chapters, what can you expect?

First, you'll learn how to distinguish between situational and internal fear. Situational fear grows out of the circumstances peculiar to the risk you're facing. It can be lessened by preparing yourself in very concrete, practical ways. Internal fear is psychological in origin. It can be reduced by following specific fear-management strategies.

Second, you will discover the internal fears you're most prone to experience. An inventory will help you identify them.

Third, you'll learn which internal fears are triggered by each of the three types of psychological risks.

Fourth, you'll see how your internal fears are magnified by negative self-talk and distorted thinking.

Finally, you'll learn specific skills for reducing and managing both situational and internal fears.

In this chapter, you will accomplish most of these objectives. In Part One, you'll learn what to do about situational fears. In Part Two, you'll measure your susceptibility to internal fears by completing an inventory. In Part Three, you'll read about the mix of internal fears that are most closely associated with self-improvement, commitment, and self-disclosure risks. In Part Four, you'll see how negative self-talk and distorted thinking make your internal fears worse.

Chapters 5 and 6 contain practical strategies for getting your internal fears under control.

Part One: Situational Fears

Imagine this: you have invented a product, a record-keeping system that makes it easy for homeowners to keep track of required home maintenance such as furnace and chimney cleaning, water system maintenance, and air conditioning service. You've talked with neighbors about your idea. You've produced a few prototypes of your record-keeping kit. Several friends have used the kits you gave them for a year, and you've gotten their feedback. As a result, you are satisfied that the home maintenance record-keeping kit is a viable product.

You see an enormous potential market for your kit and, after carefully discussing the matter with your spouse, decide to launch a business. You intend to sell your kit to homeowners throughout the United States.

You know that what you're doing is risky. A large investment will be required to test-market your product, produce it, advertise it, and so on. The more you look into the task of starting your business, the more forbidding it seems. You begin to grow genuinely afraid. You ask yourself a series of questions: How much money will be required to get underway? Where and how can I get the financing required to launch the business? How can my effort and money be spent most wisely? Can I protect my idea so larger, more established competitors can't steal it? Who will produce the product? How much inventory will I need before launching my advertising campaign? Where will I store the kits? How will I distribute them? Where will I advertise? The questions go on and on. As you come to recognize the dangers posed by wrong answers, as you realize how many things can go wrong in your planning and decision-making, your fears grow even stronger.

In that hypothetical situation, you were experiencing situational fear stemming from the actual circumstances of your risk. Your fear was an appropriate, adaptive response to a series of crucial considerations that required planning and forethought. If you failed to address them, or if you had thought of them but dismissed them, you would have been foolish. The prudent risk-taker is *not* the person who rushes blindly into a dangerous situation.

How To Respond to Situational Fear

To respond to situational fear, follow these steps:

- Identify the risk
- Identify the situational fear
- Determine what you must do or know to accomplish your objective
- Identify resources available to you
- Take action

Additional guidance is presented in Chapter 7, *How To Prepare for Taking Risks*.

Identify the risk. Write down the specific risk you want to take.

Identify the situational fear. What do you fear will happen if you take this risk? What negative consequences might follow? Why do you fear them?

Determine what you must do or know to accomplish your objective. When you thought about selling your home maintenance kit, you realized that you needed information. Your knowledge of planning, financing, and running a business was very spotty. Without the necessary information, your enterprise, regardless of the quality of the idea that inspired it, was doomed to failure. In other situations, your needs will be different.

- If you decide to enter a marathon, you need to prepare for the race by training and conditioning your body.
- If you decide to make repairs on your car, you need to know how to diagnose the problem and what to do about it.
- If you volunteer to give a speech, you need to know how to choose a topic, research it, organize your ideas, and present the talk effectively.

You may be able to meet your need by reading, talking to experts, hiring a consultant or coach, or taking similar steps. As the inventor of the home maintenance kit and the would-be entrepreneur, you might begin reading books about launching your own business. You might take a course, talk with an experienced businessperson, attend seminars, get a job with a small manufacturing company to see firsthand how things are done, or meet the need in still other ways.

You would meet your need differently under other circumstances. For example, as an aspiring marathoner, you would have to follow a training and conditioning program, perhaps under the guidance of a private coach.

Identify resources available to you. If you want to start a business and lack information, call your local library or a nearby business library and ask about resources they have on hand. Check the phone book to find the location of the nearest Small Business Administration office. Look into courses and workshops you can attend. Find out where you can hire a consultant to guide you.

If you're going to give a speech, check with a local college or adult extension service to see whether you can take a public speaking course. Contact Toastmasters International and find out whether there's a chapter nearby.

Take action. At this point in the process, you know your needs, and are familiar with the resources available to help you. The only task left is to follow through. Do the necessary reading. Consult the experts available to you. Be disciplined in your training. Take the course or courses that will help you. And so on.

Here is a chart that shows how to use these steps in two hypothetical situations.

Two Sample Responses to Situational Fear

Risk I Want To Take	*Invest $5,000 now for my child's college education in 15 years.*
Situational Fear	*I'll invest the $5,000 unwisely and either lose it altogether or wind up with too little money to send my child to college.*
What I Need To Do or Know	*I need to get information about financial planning, debt management, and investment alternatives. I need to make a budget that works around the investment.*
Resources Available to Me	*Books in the library and bookstores. Free seminars offered by my bank. My brother-in-law, the accountant. Workshops and classes in financial planning and long-term investment strategies offered at the local community college.*

Plan of Action	*During the next two weeks, I'm going to school myself in some basics, using library books; and then I'll consult with knowledgeable family and friends. After I make the investment, I'm going to take a class in financial planning — that'll help me feel confident about making this work.*

Risk I Want To Take	*I want to confront my boss about asking me to run errands for him.*
Situational Fear	*He may object to what I say, become angry, and either fire me or force me to leave my job.*
What I Need To Do or Know	*I need to figure out how to approach him and how to couch my message so that I won't offend him; I need to learn about methods of confrontation and negotiation.*
Resources Available to Me	*I can read books about confrontation and negotiation, talk with others who've been in similar predicaments, take a course or workshop. I can talk with co-workers who know my boss better than I do.*
Plan of Action	*Confront my boss by the beginning of the next fiscal year (that's in two months, so I'd better be ready by then!)*

Using one of your photocopies of the worksheet that follows, begin by choosing a particular risk you want to take. Identify the fear or fears that accompany your situation. Specify what you need to do or know to take this risk and have a successful outcome. Finally, identify the resources that are available to you in preparing to take this risk.

Worksheet: Overcoming Situational Fear

(Make several photocopies of this page, and use one worksheet for each situational fear.)

Respond to each item in the space below.

Risk I Want
To Take

Situational Fear

What I Need
To Do or Know

Resources
Available to
Me

Plan of Action

Part Two: Identifying Your Internal Fears

When your fear of risking doesn't grow out of the particular circumstances of your risk, it's the product of your own insecurities or emotional needs. Hence the label "internal fear."

When an internal fear is mild, it poses no particular obstacle to risking. But when it's extreme, it can stop you from taking chances you want to take.

For example, it's normal to fear and resist change. However, your resistance becomes excessive when it causes you to oppose a change before even considering it, no matter how minor and potentially beneficial it may be. A person who always follows a particular route to work, for example, may be closed to alternative routes, even though they might be faster or more convenient. His or her knee-jerk opposition to change borders on the extreme, as well as costing time, gasoline, and inconvenience.

In this section of the chapter, you will get to know your internal fears and how strong they are. In the next two chapters, you'll learn ways of coping with them.

Personal Fear Inventory

Below are 30 statements that describe tendencies to behave in certain ways. To what extent does each statement apply to your typical mode of behavior? Write down your score for each statement.

	Never 0	Sometimes 1	Often 2
1. I put off doing things that interest me because I'm afraid I'll fail.	_____	_____	_____
2. I settle for second best, even though a little effort would get me exactly what I want.	_____	_____	_____
3. I avoid experiences that are new and exciting because I'm afraid of making a fool of myself.	_____	_____	_____
4. I shrink from competitions in which I'd have potential to earn the success that I want.	_____	_____	_____
5. I'm a creature of habit, and resist change.	_____	_____	_____

Personal Fear Inventory

page 2

	Never 0	Sometimes 1	Often 2
6. I deliberately hold myself back from making an all-out effort in competitive situations, pretending that winning or losing doesn't really matter to me.	_____	_____	_____
7. I hesitate to ask my sex partner for some new experience out of fear that he [or she] will take offense or criticize me.	_____	_____	_____
8. In my relationships, I try to fulfill my partner's expectations instead of acting as I'd like to.	_____	_____	_____
9. Once I get into a habit, I have a hard time changing my behavior.	_____	_____	_____
10. I worry that others will reject me.	_____	_____	_____
11. I avoid confronting people who hurt me, even though I know I should.	_____	_____	_____
12. I avoid people whose opinions differ from mine.	_____	_____	_____
13. I have trouble making decisions because I'm afraid I may end up doing the wrong thing.	_____	_____	_____
14. I worry that if I were to enjoy a major success, my friends would envy me.	_____	_____	_____
15. I think of myself as "not competitive."	_____	_____	_____
16. In unfamiliar situations, I rule out certain behaviors because they're "not at all me."	_____	_____	_____

Personal Fear Inventory

page 3

	Never 0	Sometimes 1	Often 2
17. I avoid arguing with people who disagree with me, even when I'm convinced that I'm right.	_____	_____	_____
18. I avoid letting myself get too close to other people, for fear of getting hurt.	_____	_____	_____
19. My reluctance to hurt others or make them jealous makes me stop short of making my best effort to succeed.	_____	_____	_____
20. To me, regret at having made a wrong choice is among the worst things imaginable.	_____	_____	_____
21. I feel badly when the people closest to me are upset by my behavior.	_____	_____	_____
22. I avoid trying to fulfill childhood ambitions (such as learning to play a musical instrument or learning to ride a horse).	_____	_____	_____
23. I'm completely stymied by my fear that I may look back on a choice I've made and wish I'd never made it.	_____	_____	_____
24. I have a hard time leaning on other people, since I prefer to be the strong one in a relationship.	_____	_____	_____
25. I avoid striking up conversations with people who are sexually attractive to me because I'm quite certain it'll end in my being hurt.	_____	_____	_____
26. I'm easily upset by breaks in my routine.	_____	_____	_____

Personal Fear Inventory

page 4

	Never 0	Sometimes 1	Often 2
27. I prefer to play it safe when it comes to personal encounters that may end in my being rejected.	_____	_____	_____
28. I have difficulty trusting people I want to get close to.	_____	_____	_____
29. I feel guilty when I defeat someone in a game or contest, and feel unworthy of enjoying the rewards that go with victory.	_____	_____	_____
30. I avoid doing things that people look down on.	_____	_____	_____
Totals	_____	_____	_____

Scoring

Scoring your inventory will help you gauge how much your internal fears keep you from taking the risks you ought to. It will also help you identify the specific fears that hold you back.

Each response has a point value. Review your answers, tallying up the number of points you scored in each category. Write your subtotals score in the blanks at the bottom. Then tally a grand total.

Overall Score

You can interpret your overall score using the guide below:

Total Score	Overall Fear Index
0-20	Not very frightened
21-40	Moderately frightened
41-60	Very frightened

What Your Score Means

1. Score of 0-20

If your overall score is between 0 and 20, either you don't have many internal fears or you've learned ways to keep them within bounds. By completing the Personal Fear Inventory Scoresheet that follows, you can uncover any specific fears that still need your attention.

2. Score of 21-40

If you scored between 21 and 40, your internal fears keep you from risking at least some of the time. The techniques and recommendations in the next two chapters will be of interest to you.

3. Score above 40

If you scored above 40, you are severely inhibited by internal fears. You probably avoid taking chances of any kind. The material and recommendations in the next two chapters will be of vital interest to you.

How To Score the Personal Fear Inventory Scoresheet

The inventory you just completed also measures the strength of ten specific fears that may keep you from taking risks. Each one is listed on the Personal Fear Inventory Scoresheet that follows.

In the left-hand column of the scoresheet are the ten most common fears that keep people from taking risks. (A brief discussion of each fear listed appears in the "Mini-Glossary of Fears" in this chapter.) For each fear on the scoresheet, there are three corresponding statements in the inventory; these statements are listed by number in the center column of the scoresheet.

Begin with the first fear on the scoresheet: fear of failure. You'll see that questions 1, 2, and 22 measure the strength of this fear. Go back to the inventory and see what scores you got for these three questions. Next, tally up the points earned on all three of the responses that correspond to fear of failure; write the total in the right-hand column of the scoresheet. Follow the same procedure in determining your score on each of the eight other fears. Remember, the highest you can score on any one fear is 6 (two points on each of the three questions); the lowest is 0.

In arriving at your personal fear profile, keep in mind that the higher the score in the right-hand column of the scoresheet, the more pronounced your fear.

Personal Fear Inventory Scoresheet

Type of Fear	Statements on the Inventory That Measure This Fear	Total Score for This Fear
Failure	1, 2, 22	_____
Competition	4, 6, 15	_____
Disapproval in Close Relationships	7, 8, 21	_____
Generalized Disapproval	3, 16, 30	_____
Confrontation	11, 12, 17	_____
Being Wrong	13, 20, 23	_____
Change	5, 9, 26	_____
Intimacy	18, 24, 28	_____
Rejection	10, 25, 27	_____
Success	14, 19, 29	_____

In the spaces below, list the ten categories of fears, beginning with the one for which you earned the highest score — in other words, your worst fear. If you have the same score on more than one fear, list them consecutively.

My Fears

_____   _____
_____   _____
_____   _____
_____   _____
_____   _____

Look carefully at the list. The fears at the top are the ones you need to address most of all. You can gain some insight into each fear by reading about it in the Mini-Glossary of Fears that follows below. In the next two chapters, you'll learn specific strategies for managing each one.

A Mini-Glossary of Fears

Fear of Failure

This is the single most common fear that keeps people from taking risks of all kinds.

You are troubled by this fear if you associate self-worth with external success. You feel less a person if you don't succeed at what you try to accomplish. Instead of complimenting yourself for taking a risk, you punish yourself for not achieving all you could have.

Things to remember

Society values success over failure and equates failure with inadequacy. But self-worth cannot be measured by external success. You are no less a person if you don't succeed at what you try to do.

Success is a subjective perception. A teacher earning half the salary of his corporate counterpart is a success if he values his work. The fact that his profession is grossly underpaid shouldn't result in his thinking of himself as a failure.

Your worth derives from your humanity, not what you succeed at doing. Why else would we assign such enormous value to people who are helpless — such as babies — or loved relatives or friends who become sick or infirm? You are inherently valuable just because you're a human being and you're alive. Accomplishments are frosting on the cake.

If you attempt something and fail, try complimenting yourself for taking a risk instead of punishing yourself for not achieving all you could have.

People and events

- During the Persian Gulf War of 1991, Saddam Hussein suffered one of the most humiliating defeats in the history of military warfare. Nevertheless, he was hailed by many in the Arab world as a victor, because he had stood up to the United States-led coalition forces. Success, it seems, is often a matter of interpretation.

- Vincent Van Gogh never "succeeded" by conventional standards. But his achievements as a painter are in no way diminished by his failure during his lifetime to sell his work.

- Attorney Clarence Darrow failed to successfully defend a Tennessee teacher who broke with tradition by teaching students about Darwin's scientific theory of human evolution. Nevertheless, Darrow has gone down in history as discrediting fundamentalist interpretations of the Book of Genesis.

- In the early 1600s, English physician William Harvey was laughed at when he proposed his theory that the blood circulates through the body; nearly two centuries later, his theory was substantiated.

- The annals of publishing are replete with tales of books that were rejected, sometimes by scores of publishers, before finally winning acceptance and becoming block-buster best-sellers. Some examples are: *Jonathan Livingston Seagull, Zen and the Art of Motorcycle Maintenance*, and *Ordinary People*. Some classics include *Diary of Anne Frank, Lord of the Flies*, and *The Peter Principle*.

- Inventor Edwin Land failed repeatedly in his attempts to perfect the technology required to produce instant photographs. He persisted, however, and the result is the Polaroid camera.

Thoughts to ponder
- Failures in science or technology pave the way to success. Every scientific advance is built on a foundation of previous failures.

- Failure, according to industrialist H. Ross Perot, is the price successful people pay for seeking new challenges.

- The choice to become discouraged is just that: you can choose not to quit just as easily as you choose to give up.

- To the inquiring mind, more is learned from failure than from success. Paul MacCready, the father of human-powered flight (his Gossamer Condor hangs next to the Wright brothers' airplane in the Smithsonian Institution's National Air and Space Museum) has observed, "You have to try things out and accept failure as an opportunity to learn."

- If you don't try, you can't fail. But neither can you succeed.

Fear of Competition

If you avoid competition at all costs, you probably think of it in terms of winning or losing. You avoid competing to avoid the possible humiliation of losing. You see fellow competitors as enemies rather than possible allies who can help bring out your best.

The concept of the "worthy adversary" has been lost by our society. It was customary until the First World War to compliment an adversary, regardless of who the victor was. The skill and courage with which an adversary fought were acknowledged by a salute or a bow.

Things to remember

Competition doesn't only mean winning or losing; it needn't be all bound up with your ego and self-esteem. When competition serves as a motivation to do your best, it's all to the good. To avoid competition because of a fear of losing is foolish and self-defeating. Instead, throw yourself into the task and be satisfied — win or lose — that you've given it your best.

Auditioning for a part in a community theatre production or for a place in a local chorus or orchestra is inherently competitive. This is both healthy and productive. It forces aspiring performers to do their best, and weeds out those who are faint-hearted or who lack commitment.

People and events

- Tennis star John McEnroe went from being the number one player in the world to a man who was often defeated early in major tennis tournaments; but he kept on playing. He wasn't a masochist; he wasn't motivated by a desire to lose. Rather, his intent was to play the best he could, not simply to win.

- The space race, a healthy competition between the United States and the former Soviet Union, challenged scientists in both countries to press themselves and their technologies to their limits. The results benefit mankind every day, and will do so in the future in ways we can hardly imagine now.

Thoughts to ponder

- In free market economies, competition is in everyone's best interest. It forces manufacturers and service providers to improve operating efficiencies, keep production and service delivery costs low, and improve quality. Ultimately, the consumer benefits.

- The best athletes in the world risk defeat in every competition they enter. Yet they wouldn't have it any other way. Without competition, they wouldn't be driven to achieve excellence.

- Game theorists say that all contests — whether in politics, sports, or business — require a fine balance between competition and cooperation.

- American essayist Henry David Thoreau wrote, "Life is a battle in which we are to show our pluck, and woe be to the coward."

- Competitive situations shouldn't be seen as a way to vent aggression, but rather as an opportunity to achieve your personal best.

- For people who feel secure in their sense of self-worth, competition is a way of testing themselves and gauging their efforts — not a means of asserting their superiority over others. In other words, the most valid competition is always within yourself.

- There are few situations in the world in which the theory of "limited good" applies. The fact that someone else succeeds at something you'd like to do doesn't mean that your chances are now diminished. Someone else's accomplishment can, in fact, serve as an inspiration.

Fear of Disapproval in Close Relationships

If you are especially subject to this fear, your self-esteem may be tenuous. You believe you're only as nice or good as your intimates think you are. As a result, you take your cue from them: What do they want? What would please them? What would upset them? In asking such questions, you fail to take into account your own wants and needs. If you maintain such thinking for long periods of time, you eventually lose yourself and no longer know what you want, how you feel, or even who you are.

Things to remember
To stay in touch with yourself, spend less time worrying about what others want and more time thinking about what you want yourself. Practice making decisions based on your own intuitions and feelings; be very clear about your own preferences.

People and events
- Popular singer Neil Diamond was expected to follow in his father's footsteps and become a cantor in his synagogue. He had to overcome the disapproval of his family to accomplish his personal goal.

- Countless actors, athletes, and writers have achieved success in spite of the opposition of parents and family.

Thoughts to ponder
- You can't move forward without leaving something behind. This "something" may be a place, people you care about, or a way of life.

- One of the most important and difficult jobs parents have is to let a child become what he or she wants to be, rather than imposing their own desires and values.

- You will ultimately respect yourself more if you pursue your dreams rather than foregoing them out of a sense of fear, duty, or sacrifice. You will also be a nicer person to know.

- It's unrealistic to expect every choice you make to win the approval of the people closest to you.

- If you think only of others first, you may forget how to get in touch with your own needs and feelings.

Generalized Fear of Disapproval

If you scored high in this category, your fear of disapproval extends to just about anyone with whom you come into contact. To avoid risking their displeasure, you assume a low profile and avoid "making waves." No matter who you deal with — the clerk in the grocery store, the gas station attendant, the receptionist in the doctor's office — you strive to be "nice," inoffensive, likable. Your need for approval is indiscriminate. Generally, you believe that you are only as nice or attractive as other people think you are.

Things to remember

The disapproval of others is more a function of their inner world than any reflection on you or your actions. You aren't responsible for others' feelings. You simply are who you are; others respond to you with a full array of private prejudices and distractions. Often people sense disapproval where none is intended: another person's frown probably has nothing to do with you at all, but is more a function of that person's inner thoughts (or indigestion!).

People and Events

- Before starting the Protestant Reformation, Martin Luther was among the most fervent of monks. Openly challenging the authority of the Church required extreme courage in the face of disapproval.

- Creative geniuses throughout history have known that their ideas might evoke scornful responses from their professional colleagues — Sigmund Freud comes to mind as a prime example. But they pushed on anyway, risking disapproval, scorn, rejection, and humiliation, out of their belief in the soundness of their ideas.

Thoughts to ponder

- In the first century B.C., Pubilius Syrus observed, "It is a very hard undertaking to seek to please everybody."

- You don't exist to gratify others.

- To live your life as a collection of mirrors, reflecting what others think you should be, is not to live at all.

Fear of Confrontation

If this is at the top of your list, you dread any head-on confrontation with another person. You may fear the other person's anger, or feel horrified at the thought of hurting someone's feelings. On the other hand, you may simply be afraid of coming off badly in an argument. Because of this dread, you'll probably accept shoddy treatment rather than risk making a scene. Afterwards, you may despise yourself for being a wimp. As other people catch on to your lack of assertiveness, they'll tend to take advantage of you or treat you contemptuously in any number of situations. It's almost as if you're wearing a sign that says, "I won't fight back — go ahead and push me around!"

Things to remember

Confrontation is often necessary. After all, the world isn't set up to satisfy your particular needs. If you never let people know how you feel or what you want, chances are that you're going to wind up feeling hurt and dissatisfied a lot of the time.

When it's well planned, confrontation is almost always beneficial for all parties involved. It clears the air and lets everyone know where you stand and "what's going on." People who live and work with you will be grateful to know how you feel and what pleases you, so that they can stop trying to read your mind. Don't forget — other people also crave acceptance and approval! At the very least, facing another person head on can sharpen your skills and build your confidence.

There's no reason to fear confrontations. If you've thought a situation through carefully, know your goals, anticipate the other person's reactions, and are prepared for "worst-case" scenarios, the odds are strongly in favor of your succeeding.

People and events

- Adult victims of date rape often report that their biggest mistake was not confronting their assailant early in the sexual encounter. Not wanting to make a scene proved a major factor in their victimization.

- "Yes-men" and appeasers made it possible for Hitler to launch the horrors of World War II.

- According to Robert Townsend, former Chief Executive Officer of the Avis car rental agency and author of *Up the Organization,* the most valuable friend a company executive can have is a subordinate who will "tell it like it is." At Avis, Townsend's personal "crap detector" helped him avoid many blunders.

Thoughts to ponder

- Justice is largely the result of a willingness to confront injustice.

- You owe it to others you care for to let them in on what you want and how you feel.

- You will almost always learn something useful from a confrontation, both about yourself and the other person or people involved. You are also teaching others something about yourself. A confrontation is an exchange of information.

Fear of Being Wrong

Perhaps your fear of being wrong or regretting your decisions causes you to hesitate whenever you have to make a choice that has important consequences. This hesitation may be especially pronounced when the choice has immediate, practical consequences. For example, you may hesitate unreasonably when making an investment decision for fear of losing money or not maximizing your gain. Or you may remain silent out of a fear of saying the wrong thing: your silence may cost you dearly in terms of your relationships with people you love.

The fear of being wrong is especially poignant when you have limited resources and can't "hedge your bets." This is also keenly felt when a choice you make precludes all others. For example, when you marry, you choose one partner to the exclusion of others. It's the same, in a shorter timeframe, when you choose to accept a job. The fear of being wrong may result in the loss of wonderful opportunities.

If you are especially troubled by the fear of being wrong, chances are that you want guarantees that are simply not possible.

Things to remember

When making complex choices, you must rely on probabilities, since certainties don't exist in this world (apart from death and taxes). Nevertheless, it's wise to try to reduce uncertainty as far as you can. For example, if you were planning to buy a specific kind of car, you'd be wise to consult consumer magazines to learn about its reliability and how well other owners have liked it. At a certain point, however, information-gathering has to give way to that moment of risk when you make your decision. There will always be an element of risk, no matter how much information you have.

Many of the most agonizing social decisions faced by people today — whom to marry, whether to have children, what sort of career to pursue — weren't matters of choice in the not-so-distant past. Your parents decided whom you would marry, children followed or didn't according to the dictates of nature, and you probably went into the same line of work as your father (if you were a woman, you either did hard agricultural labor or didn't work at all outside the home). It's important to remember that people survive, and even manage to find pleasure in life, no matter how these decisions are cast.

People and events

- The American Civil Liberties Union (ACLU) regularly evokes the wrath of both left-wing and right-wing extremists, because it defends with equal vigor citizens at both ends of the political spectrum. Unfailing adherence to the principle of civil liberties (and not a particular political agenda) is the guiding force in the ACLU's actions.

- The Greek philosopher Aristotle argued that it's often necessary to base our thinking on probabilities, since absolute certainty is not possible.

- Creative innovators such as Walt Disney, investors such as Malcolm Forbes, and medical pioneers such as Marie Curie went ahead with their dreams, not because they were certain they would succeed, but because they were satisfied that the odds were in favor of success.

Thoughts to ponder

- The desire for certainty is a futile quest; the more we seek it, the more it eludes us.

- In the real world, there are few decisions that can't be questioned.

- There are also few decisions — apart from suicide, murder, or the birth of a child — that can't, in the long term, be changed.

Fear of Change

If fear of change rated high for you in the personal inventory of fears, you crave stability and sameness, and dread breaks in your routine. You go to great lengths to avoid risking your security. You find change to be threatening. Your identity and self-esteem are bound up with your surroundings; you've built your security around predictable events and behaviors.

Things to remember

Stability, sameness, and routine provide a measure of security that almost everyone craves. Society abhors "drifters": pleasurable routine is the cornerstone of happiness for most people. Yet, when carried to an extreme, the dictates of routine can be stultifying. If you're too rigid, you risk missing many of the satisfactions that can be afforded by work, travel, recreation, and social interaction.

Many changes at first glance appear threatening and unsettling: the loss of a job, an eviction, the end of a relationship. And yet all such changes can serve as cosmic kicks in the butt to go on to different — and better — things. Try to view change as an opportunity to open yourself to new experiences.

People and events

- The Constitution of the United States provides for mandated change by limiting the number of terms a President can serve: new ideas and new leadership are essential to the health of the nation.

- John Gardner is former head of the Department of Health, Education, and Welfare, and founder of the citizen's lobby, Common Cause. He maintains in his book, *Self-Renewal*, that unless a society actively promotes change from within, it will fail to renew itself and slowly die. Constitutional guarantees of free speech, he argues, reflect an awareness that a society can only renew itself when it protects those innovators who bring fresh ideas into the public consciousness.

- Many successful organizations operate on the principle that it's a mistake to wait until change is forced on the system from the outside; instead, they regularly survey the external environment, examine their internal processes, and initiate change from within. For instance, a school district is more likely to serve students better when teachers and administrators examine the community they serve and make curricular and structural changes to better meet its needs.

Thoughts to ponder

- In his teaching and writing, Fritz Perls, a distinguished psychiatrist and founder of Gestalt Therapy, made a crucial distinction between static security and dynamic security. The former, he says in *Gestalt Therapy Verbatim*, is the security that comes from clinging to what is known and familiar. It is an inferior form of adjustment, and ultimately results in a reduced capacity to adapt to the demands of reality. By contrast, dynamic security is never fixed but always in the making. It comes from a willingness to sacrifice static security, confident that a new and better balance can be achieved, According to Perls, static security is the security of death; dynamic security is the security of life.

- In the fifth century B.C., the Greek philosopher Heraclitus observed, "Nothing endures but change." It's futile to resist change, as change is inevitable in any living system. It's far wiser to embrace change, affirm it, and even initiate it — to adjust change to your needs as much as possible.

Fear of Intimacy

Perhaps the idea of getting close to someone is very frightening for you. Do you usually keep your distance from others, and feel very ambivalent when you begin to become emotionally involved? If you can't maintain a distance, you may try to control the people you're close to: the unpredictability in their behavior makes you feel vulnerable. No one likes feeling pushed away or controlled: you probably have difficulty establishing and maintaining close relationships.

Things to remember

The rewards associated with getting close to someone almost always outweigh the risks. By distancing yourself from others and trying to control them when they get too close, you make satisfying intimate relationships impossible.

Bad experiences with people — an alcoholic or abusive partner, for example — are awful enough in themselves. But when you permit them to discourage you from having any close relationships at all, you actually promote your own victimization. The solution is to overcome resistance by permitting yourself to become involved with others while simultaneously ensuring that you don't repeat the mistakes of the past. This will require vigilance on your part, and may require professional assistance.

People and events

- Toward the end of his life, industrialist Howard Hughes sank into insanity as he isolated himself from virtually everyone. The sad ending to this otherwise successful life shows the result of fear of intimacy when carried to its logical extreme.

- One person we knew kept her distance from the men she met by spinning fantastic yarns about her job, her past experiences, and her lifestyle. A nurse who lived comfortably but quietly, she created a fantasy self, telling male acquaintances that she was a former airline pilot who earned her living as an international consultant to the airline industry. When she took trips out of town (in reality she attended meetings of her professional associations), she claimed to be in Europe, the Far East, or other exotic places. While her pretense helped her feel safe and less vulnerable, it also virtually guaranteed that no relationship she formed would ever mature: she had to maintain her distance to maintain the lie.

Thoughts to ponder

- Intimacy, vulnerability, and growth are inextricably connected. When you refuse to make yourself vulnerable, you turn your back on growth and intimacy.

- There are two alternatives to intimacy: loneliness and manipulation. The first results from the refusal to form ties with others. The second is the result of an overly strong need to protect yourself by controlling others.

- Psychiatrist Eric Berne, author of the classic book *Games People Play*, noted that psychological games — predictable interpersonal patterns by which people satisfy each others' need to relate — are a sort of meringue: they look and feel like intimacy and provide some of its satisfactions, but are without substance. It was his hope and his purpose when he worked with patients to help people experience the profound joys of genuine intimacy.

Fear of Rejection

Some people fear rejection even more than death. If you're among this category of people, you're quick to blame yourself if others reject you. You probably attribute any rejection to your failure to be appealing, agreeable, or lovable. This fear is strongly related to the fear of confrontation discussed earlier. It's crucial for you to realize that the reasons for a person's rejection of you may have little or nothing to do with you at all.

Even if your behavior does contribute to a rejection, the most constructive response you can have is to identify the problematic behavior and work to change it. Self-blame will only undermine your confidence and diminish your attractiveness as a companion, co-worker, or friend.

Things to remember

No one ever scored a significant success, interpersonal or otherwise, without first experiencing a number of rejections. It's unrealistic to expect that everyone will like you or respond to your ideas, even after a number of tries.

A certain randomness operates whenever you set out to win the acceptance of others. If you catch them in a good mood, in the middle of a good day, you'll find that gaining acceptance is easy. Under the opposite circumstances, nothing you could do would win the acceptance you want. There's an entire subconscious network of associations that determines one individual's response from another: these are entirely out of your control. All you can do is present your best self and hope that chemistry and memory conspire to your advantage.

People who judge others harshly — and reject them — are sometimes quite unhappy with themselves and their lives. It's a mistake to allow these negative, self-hating people to poison your attitudes and undermine your confidence.

People and events

- Lee Iacocca has written eloquently about the loss of his job as President of the Ford Motor Company. He was fired after spearheading the development of the hugely successful Mustang, following two consecutive years of record earnings for which Iacocca was largely responsible. Despite the bitter personal circumstances surrounding the loss of his job, Iacocca refused to be cowed by the experience. Instead, he resolved to outdo his former boss, Henry Ford, Jr. — and that's what he did as CEO at Chrysler.

- Clara McBride Hale grew up in poverty, the youngest of four children, in Philadelphia, Pennsylvania. Widowed at 27, she was left with three children, all below the age of eight. After her husband's death, she worked as a domestic — cleaning homes by day and theatres by night — just to put food on the table. She not only raised her own three children, but in her later years opened Hale House, in Harlem, where she cared for babies born to drug-addicted mothers.

- Edith Wharton, one of America's outstanding novelists, suffered numerous rejections before going on to write her classic work, *Ethan Frome*, and the Pulitzer Prize-winning novel, *The Age of Innocence*.

- Although Elizabeth Cady Stanton, nineteenth century feminist and social reformer, was unquestionably brilliant, she was denied the opportunity to pursue higher education and enter a profession simply because she was female. Rather than shrinking in the face of rejection, or resigning herself to a life of domestic anonymity, she used her outrage to champion women's rights. Together with the likes of Susan B. Anthony, Stanton became one of the foremost social activists of her time.

Thoughts to ponder

- If your self-esteem depends entirely on what others think of you, you haven't got any.

- If someone rejects you, the rejection is as much a product of what that person brings to the relationship as it is a reaction to you or your behavior.

- Persistence in the face of rejection is what distinguishes effective people from mediocre ones in every profession.

- Successful salespeople know better than to be discouraged by rejection. To them, every rejection brings them one step closer to acceptance.

- It's often a mistake, and almost always useless, to take rejection personally.

- Novelist and diarist Anaïs Nin cautioned, "Beware of allowing a tactless word, a rebuttal, a rejection to obliterate the whole sky."

- There is a principle in career counseling that is intended to guide people who have lost their jobs: for every $7,000 of salary, a person should expect to look for a job for one month. Thus, a person earning $70,000 per year should expect to accumulate ten months' worth of rejections before finding a position equivalent to the one he or she had before.

Fear of Success

It may be that you undermine your success because you fear its consequences: jealousy, loss of friends, loneliness. Rather than risk being too successful, you may consciously stop yourself from making an all-out effort, or unconsciously undermine your performance. In the end, you achieve less than you can — and you may end up feeling badly about it, too.

Central to the fear of success is a tendency to assume responsibility for the feelings of others. Your thinking runs something like this: "If, in reaction to my success, someone else feels resentful or envious, their feelings are my fault."

On the face of it, this notion is absurd.

People are responsible for their own feelings (this includes you!). If you have friends who depend on your lack of success for their happiness, then you need to find some new friends.

Thinking that you are at the center of everyone's world can greatly exaggerate your notions about other people's envy. Most people are too involved with their own lives to care much one way or the other about your success or failure. These are assessments that must be nurtured, judged, and respected by you and you alone.

Things to remember

Your success doesn't need to bring about the adverse consequences you fear. By developing your abilities fully and achieving all that you can, you're showing respect for your gifts as a human being, and providing a healthy role model for others. Everyone suffers in the end when a person sacrifices his or her talents on the altar of modesty or martyrdom. Such sacrifices seem to undergo a chemical change over the years, turning into bitterness, resentment, and anger.

People and events

- Fear of success shows itself whenever a person repeatedly reaches the threshold of success, but doesn't cross it. From that person's point of view, "things just seem to happen" to prevent the success from occurring. For example, a student who has been doing extremely well in a course suddenly stops attending, or fails to complete a required assignment. Asked why, the student will point to "circumstances" without assuming responsibility for the decision not to succeed.

Thoughts to ponder

- Sometimes people feel guilty if they exceed the accomplishments of their parents, especially in the case of women and their mothers and men and their fathers. If you find yourself sabotaging your success, it may be worthwhile to examine whether your feelings about your parents enter into the equation. Such issues are best explored either in individual or group therapy with a qualified counselor.

- Success is a matter of definition. To a spectator, an Olympic athlete who fails to win a gold medal might be considered a loser — especially in light of all the effort that made participation in the Olympics possible. However, to the athlete, the opportunity to have participated represents a success, regardless of medals won.

- The statement "all men are created equal" does not mean that everyone is equally talented and intelligent: it means simply they're equal before the law. It is both wrong and foolish to deny your God-given talents.

Part Three: Internal Fears Associated With Each Type of Psychological Risk

Each type of psychological risk triggers — and is inhibited by — specific fears. Self-improvement risks are typically associated with fear of failure. Commitment risks are most often associated with fear of being wrong. And self-disclosure risks are ordinarily associated with fear of rejection, disapproval, or confrontation.

Although each type of psychological risk can be strongly associated with a specific fear, a simple one-to-one correlation doesn't exist. Each particular risk sparks a unique constellation of fears. In the examples below, the fear most closely associated with each type of risk is discussed first, followed by related fears that we also associated with that risk.

Internal Fears Associated With Self-Improvement Risks

The fact that self-improvement risks are often inhibited by a fear of failure isn't surprising, since these risks usually involve "stretching yourself" — putting yourself on the line in some way.

Dana had made a successful career for herself in advertising, but had always dreamed of being a novelist. When she was 52, she inherited some money — enough to allow her to quit her job for a couple of years. This was the opportunity that Dana had always been waiting for. And yet she kept putting off giving her notice at the advertising agency, finding one excuse after another. Finally, when several years had gone by, she rationalized that she'd be foolish not to wait until her retirement instead of quitting — then she'd be guaranteed a lifetime income, not just an income for one or two years.

But when retirement did come and Dana received her pension and her gold watch, she found herself crippled with a terrible sense of angst every time she rolled a blank sheet of paper into her typewriter. Several months later, she began to have bone pain so severe that it kept her awake at night. The doctors diagnosed her as suffering from rheumatoid arthritis.

With the help of a therapist and some soul-searching, Dana realized that she was mortally terrified of finding out just how much — or how little — talent she had. Her dreams and expectations had built up to the point where producing anything less than the great American novel would have felt like a crushing failure.

Dana decided that she *had* to overcome her fear; and one way to do this seemed to be to set her sights a little lower. She decided to start writing short stories, not even with an eye to publication, but just to see whether she could harness her intelligence and creativity in the fictional mode. After a year of laborious work with a tape recorder and a secretary (by this time, Dana's fingers were too crippled to allow her to type), Dana showed her collection of stories to a friend who was a literary agent. Without even telling her, he started sending out her stories to literary magazines; four of the stories were accepted immediately. These were followed by an offer from an East Coast publisher to print the entire collection.

Dana likes to say that it took her a lifetime to do it — she's 70 now — but she's finally fulfilled her dream of being a novelist: her first novel was published last year, and was received with warm praise by the critics. The funny thing is that her arthritis flare-ups have become more and more infrequent, to the point where she can do most of her composing on the typewriter herself.

Fear of failure may lurk behind your reluctance to take self-improvement risks. But other fears may play a part as well. Ironically, one of them is the fear of success.

Paul was a middle manager who'd worked for a large corporation since graduating from college. His work was good, and his career had progressed nicely over a period of several years. Any further advancement would have required a significant increase in his responsibilities. At this point in his career, however, Paul began behaving in ways that were uncharacteristic of him: arriving late for meetings, missing deadlines, failing to have information on hand that he knew would be required. Worse still, he volunteered for special projects — something he had always done and carried off admirably — only now he was failing to see them through.

These behaviors were so uncharacteristic of Paul that his boss took him aside and spoke with him at length. The conversation initially caused Paul to become upset; he felt as though he were being attacked and discredited. But when it became clear that Paul's boss really wanted him to get ahead, Paul had to begin thinking seriously about what was going on. Over time he came to realize that he was ambivalent about further advancement of his career. As much as he wanted to get ahead, he was afraid he might not be able to handle the increased responsibilities. He recognized in time that his ambivalence found expression in his failing to perform his job adequately. When Paul overcame his fear of success, his career was able to advance.

Self-improvement risks can also spark a fear of disapproval and rejection. One young woman, a college sophomore, wanted to be a model. Jeannie was willowy and attractive. A lover of fashion, she had always been drawn to the theatrics and glamor of modeling. An opportunity came along for her to compete for an assignment. But when she shared her good fortune with her parents, they were decidedly unenthusiastic. "You don't want to become a model," they said. "It's sleazy! It's superficial! What will you do with your life after you lose your good looks?"

Jeannie was torn. She wanted a career in modeling more than almost anything. Yet she loved her parents and was haunted by the thought of their disapproval.

The fear of competition can inhibit self-improvement risks. George was a terrific artist who had sold a lot of his work; but a fear of not measuring up to "real" artists kept him from submitting slides of his work to a juried competition.

A fear of change can be sparked by self-improvement risks. Andrea was a college teacher who had spent her life in the shadow of her older sister, who was a high-powered corporate attorney. All her life, Andrea was used to living in her sister's shadow: she didn't see herself as someone capable of assuming important responsibilities beyond the day-to-day duties of teaching and research. Whenever a problem arose in her department, Andrea instinctively looked around for an older, more powerful person to handle it.

After many years of behaving this way, the survival of her academic department was thrown into question by an arbitrary administrative action. Since the basis of the action tied in with Andrea's special area of competence, the responsibility for defending her department fell logically on Andrea's shoulders. She panicked: how could she be expected to save the whole department by herself?

Andrea realized that mustering the courage to lead her department under these circumstances would necessitate dramatic change in her long-standing behavior and attitudes about herself. The fear of changing the status quo almost kept Andrea from doing what had to be done. But when she pushed through the fear, she managed to rise to the occasion in a manner worthy of her brilliant and aggressive big sister. She had never guessed at the depth of her own resourcefulness and strength.

Internal Fears Associated With Commitment Risks

Once again, the fear most closely associated with commitment risks is the fear of being wrong.

Cora got her Ph.D. in biology and began her career working for a biotechnology firm. Two years later, she married. She and her husband both wanted a family. They waited a while, and Cora's career advanced. Then they decided to try to conceive. Four months later, she found herself pregnant. Cora was elated. Yet she knew she would face a crossroad once the child was born. Should she leave the baby with a caretaker and continue working as soon as she was physically able; or should she leave her job — perhaps take an extended leave of absence — and stay home to care for the baby herself? She knew that the high-paced field of biotechnology didn't wait around for scientists on maternity leave; and she and her team were on the verge of a breakthrough.

Cora's dilemma centered around a commitment risk: to which of the two values — career or family — should she commit herself?

The fear of committing yourself to the wrong value can pose a serious obstacle to risk-taking. The truth is, there is no objectively "correct" answer in such cases as Cora's. No one can ever predict with certainty which choice is correct. What matters, ultimately, is the subjective preferences of the person making the commitment: you're the one who will have to live with your choice.

Commitment risks can also spark — and be inhibited by — the fear of disapproval or rejection. You may elect to stand up for a principle you believe in, knowing full well that others, who don't happen to share your value system, will think you foolish or worse. Take the case of Barry, the adolescent child of a doctor and a college teacher. Always gifted with his hands, Barry loved cars and could think of nothing more satisfying than learning about them in depth. But he knew that if he were to choose trade school over college, he would devastate his parents. In the end, he did precisely that, risking their rejection and disapproval. It was, after all, his life and career that were at stake.

Fear of change can inhibit commitment risks. Sometimes commitments require major changes. For example, a young person accustomed to living in luxury who decides to follow a religious vocation or join the Peace Corps would certainly have to accept the changes dictated by such a choice.

Commitment risks are often accompanied by a fear of success. Like failure, success also has its consequences. Will you feel like a fraud if you succeed? Will your friends feel jealous? Will your spouse feel abandoned or eclipsed? And what will happen to all the comforts of your old way of life if your wildest fantasy suddenly comes true? Such fears can cause you to sabotage your own success.

Internal Fears Associated With Self-Disclosure Risks

Whether you declare your love for someone, or assertively confront a friend, co-worker, or family member, you run the risk of disapproval, rejection, or both.

Like commitment risks, self-disclosure may be accompanied by the fear of success. People who break free of unhealthy and manipulative relationships, for example, invariably confront many unanticipated changes. They must make their own choices rather than giving that responsibility to others. Assuming control also means giving up your usual excuses for not trying — all those "circumstances," and all that manipulation by others. While such changes are, in the end, beneficial, they can nevertheless be terrifying.

Self-disclosure risks may spark a fear of intimacy. When you declare your love for someone, you must be prepared to face the possibility that he or she may love you in return. Are you ready for that? The prospect of immediate intimacy and commitment can feel much more daunting than a daydream of unrequited love.

Fear of confrontation can be stirred up by self-disclosure risks. It's impossible to predict how someone is going to respond to you when you speak your mind. One possibility is that your self-disclosure will lead to a nasty confrontation. Roy, for instance, really wanted to tell his father that he was gay. But he couldn't get over the fear that his dad would respond by rejecting him. Roy loved his father and was very afraid of losing him.

Part Four: Negative Self-Talk and Cognitive Distortions

Jan had been seeing a therapist for a year when she complained of the side effects of her anti-depressant medication. She was doing well in therapy; she'd made several important changes in her life. Perhaps, she proposed, it was time to begin withdrawing from the medication.

After in-depth discussion of the issue, Jan and her therapist made an appointment with the psychiatrist who had originally prescribed the antidepressant for her. Together, they explained why it seemed an appropriate time for Jan to begin tapering off the drugs.

The psychiatrist spoke with Jan at some length. He determined that her request was a reasonable one, and agreed to have her begin gradually reducing the medication.

Jan showed signs of distress as the psychiatrist explained the process of withdrawing from the medication. He paused and asked her what was the matter. A long silence followed, then Jan started to cry. "I'm really excited about this," she said, "but I'm also afraid." "Of what?" the psychiatrist asked her. "Afraid I'll fail," said Jan. The psychiatrist offered reassurances. After all, if she followed the appropriate withdrawal schedule, how could she fail? "I'll find a way," murmured Jan.

Jan's final comment says a great deal about the way people nurture and magnify their fears. Some fear is quite understandable in a situation like Jan's. It's logical for her to question what role her medication has played in her recovery, and whether she might experience a relapse if the medication is withdrawn. But Jan magnified these reasonable fears in two ways: negative self-talk and cognitive distortion.

Negative self-talk is the phrase used to describe the self-sabotaging chatter that goes on inside people's heads. When Jan murmured that she'd find a way to fail, she revealed the pattern of negative self-talk that had magnified her fear of getting off the antidepressive medication. Self-talk exists unnoticed, for the most part, like the sound of a waterfall behind your thoughts. And yet what you say to yourself in this background monologue has a powerful effect on your perceptions and feelings. When the voice inside your head says, "I don't deserve to succeed," or "Of course I'll fail," you tend to believe it. It's only by becoming aware of your self-talk that you can hope to change the message to something more positive. This will be discussed in detail later in the book.

Jan was also feeding her fears by convincing herself that she'd find a way to fail! This was a cognitive distortion: one of several patterns of thinking that twists reality, usually in a way that makes you come out looking bad.

The table below shows the chain of connections between the nine main types of internal fears and the negative self-talk that feeds them. A detailed explanation of the cognitive distortions listed here follows later in the book. You'll also learn later how to purge negative self-talk from your inner vocabulary.

This fear	is most likely fed by this kind of negative self-talk	and is the product of these cognitive distortions	and probably discourages you from taking these risks
Fear of Failure	*I'll make a fool of myself and everyone will laugh at me.*	Labeling, Fortune-telling	Self-improvement (for example, trying out for a part in a play)
	I'm not good at new things.	Overgeneralization	Self-improvement (for example, learning a new skill)
	I'll never succeed.	All-or-nothing thinking	Self-disclosure (for example, confronting a supervisor about playing favorites)
Fear of Competition	*I'll probably lose and appear foolish.*	Fortune-telling	Self-improvement (for example, entering a dance contest)
	I'm not a winner. I'm certainly not competitive.	Labeling	Self-improvement (for example, challenging a friend to a round of golf)
Fear of Disapproval	*They'll be upset with me. They'll never understand.*	Mind reading, All-or-nothing thinking	Self-disclosure (for example, disagreeing with a family value)
	I'll come across as strident or overbearing.	Mind reading, Fortune-telling, Labeling	Commitment (for example, joining a radical political party)
Fear of Confrontation	*My voice will shake and I'll make a fool of myself.*	Fortune-telling, Labeling	Self-disclosure (for example, confronting your boss about your work load)
	I can never find the right words.	Overgeneralization	Self-disclosure (for example, asking a co-worker to pay back the money he owes you)

This fear	is most likely fed by this kind of negative self-talk	and is the product of these cognitive distortions	and probably discourages you from taking these risks
Fear of Being Wrong	*If I make a mistake, the results will be disastrous.*	Catastrophizing	Self-improvement (for example, choosing one investment vehicle over another)
	I'll probably regret my action.	Fortune-telling	Commitment (for example, quitting a job because of sexual harassment)
Fear of Change	*If I try to change, I'll fall on my face.*	Fortune-telling	Self-improvement (for example, moving away from home, finding a new job)
	Nobody will accept the new me.	Mind reading	Commitment (for example, deciding to buy a toupee)
Fear of Intimacy	*I'll get hurt if I let others get too close to me.*	Fortune-telling	Commitment (for example, committing oneself to an exclusive love relationship)
	When he gets to know me, he'll lose interest.	Mind reading	Self-disclosure (for example, starting a new relationship)
	People can't be trusted.	Overgeneralization	Self-disclosure (for example, inviting a co-worker home for a beer after work)
Fear of Rejection	*People always wind up rejecting.*	Overgeneralization	Self-disclosure (for example, challenging a superior at work)
	If I'm rejected I'll die!	Catastrophizing	Commitment (for example, proposing marriage)

This fear	is most likely fed by this kind of negative self-talk	and is the product of these cognitive distortions	and probably discourages you from taking these risks
			Self-improvement (for example, trying out for a part in a play)
Fear of Success	*If I achieve my goal, I'll never be able to live up to people's expectations.*	Fortune-telling	Self-improvement (for example, selling a business idea to a group of investors)
	If I succeed, I'll lose my friends and be lonely for the rest of my life.	Fortune-telling; Catastrophizing	Self-improvement (for example, going back to school)
			Commitment (for example, supporting an unpopular cause)

In the next two chapters, you'll learn practical strategies for managing your internal fears.

Further Reading

Berne, E. (1964) *Games People Play*. New York: Ballantine Books.

Gardner, J. (1965) *Self-Renewal*. New York: Harper-Colophon Books.

Keyes, R. (1985) *Chancing It*. Boston: Little, Brown and Company.

Nin, A. (1969) *The Diary of Anaïs Nin*, Volume III. San Diego, CA: Harcourt Brace Jovanovich.

Perls, F. (1969) *Gestalt Therapy Verbatim*. Moab, Utah: Real People Press.

Townsend, R. (1970) *Up the Organization*. New York: Alfred A. Knopf.

5

Overcoming Your Fear
of Risk-Taking
by Shaping Your Behavior

You now have a clear idea of the risks you avoid taking. You've also identified the fears that keep you from taking these risks. It's time to begin overcoming those fears.

You'll learn two ways: systematic desensitization (developed by Dr. Joseph Wolpe of the Eastern Pennsylvania Psychiatric Institute) and the threshold method (described by Doctors Spencer A. Rathus and Jeffrey S. Nevid).

Both techniques work by gradually reducing your fear through well-planned activities. In each, you proceed methodically through a series of steps, each bringing you closer to the situation you fear.

Technique One: Desensitization

Before you can desensitize yourself successfully, you need to learn how to achieve a state of relaxation. You will be returning to that state each time you become fearful on the way toward your goal.

There are three time-tested relaxation methods. All share a common premise: relaxation is a skill that can be learned, like playing the guitar or learning to cook.

Relaxation Method One: Progressive Self-Relaxation (PSR)

This technique involves alternately tensing and relaxing different muscle groups until you work your way through the body and achieve a state of complete relaxation.

The muscle groups tensed and relaxed are: hands and wrists; biceps, triceps, and upper forearms; forehead and mid-face region, mouth region, neck region, shoulders, abdomen, buttocks, thighs, calves, and feet.

Here are the rules to follow when doing PSR:

1. Do *not* practice PSR without consulting your physician first, especially if you are suffering from any current back problems, respiratory difficulties, or muscle sprains.

2. Before beginning PSR, be certain that the setting is private, comfortable, and distraction-free. Disconnect the phone or turn on your answering machine. Instruct your family or others at home not to disturb you. (If possible, avoid predictable distractions. For example, do your PSR before the children come home from school.) The room you're in should not be overly bright. Subdued lighting is desirable.

3. Find a comfortable place to lie down, or sit in a stable reclining chair.

4. PSR requires that you listen to detailed instructions (see the instructions later in this chapter). There are two sets of instructions provided. The longer set is for the first two weeks of your training. After that, you'll be able to use the abbreviated instructions. You can memorize both sets of instructions if you're good at memorizing; or record them on tape and play them back during your relaxation sessions. If you make a recording, remember to vary your tone of voice. Use a firm but not harsh tone of voice to focus on a tensed muscle group. When you're telling yourself to relax, make your voice soothing. Be sure to leave pauses of several seconds each time you tell yourself to tense your muscles. Pause for about half a minute each time you invite yourself to allow the relaxation to spread (see item 8 further in these instructions). If you want to, you can record instructions with soft music playing in the background.

   A third option is to have a friend or family member read the relaxation script to you. This requires a considerable investment of time on their part. It also requires that you sacrifice privacy. Nevertheless, you may find this arrangement suitable. If you do choose this option, be sure that you show these instructions to your reader.

Finally, you may want to purchase professionally recorded relaxation tapes. Such tapes are available from a number of sources. Four outlets include:

- Big Sur Recordings, P.O. Box 91, Big Sur, CA 93920

- Cognetics, Box 592, Saratoga, CA 95070

- New Harbinger Publications, Inc., 5674 Shattuck Avenue, Oakland, CA 94609

- Whole Person Press, P.O. Box 3151, Duluth, MN 55803

If your local hospital offers a stress management course or workshop, ask whether prerecorded tapes are available. (Consider taking a course in stress management as a way to learn several additional relaxation techniques.)

5. Never tense any part of your body so much that it hurts. You should feel a gentle to moderate tension, but no more.

6. Hold the contraction for several seconds. Breathe in comfortably as you contract each muscle group. Focus your attention on the sensations.

7. Relax the contraction all at once, not in stages. Exhale as you do so. Focus on the contrast between the relaxed sensations and the tense ones.

8. Pause for about thirty seconds after each release of tension. Enjoy the feeling of relaxation. Allow it to spread throughout your body.

9. Follow the full-length PSR instructions twice a day for two weeks. Allow about thirty-five minutes initially for each relaxation session.

After two weeks, follow the abbreviated instructions twice daily. After you become familiar with the procedure, you'll be able to complete the abbreviated form of PSR in around five minutes.

Don't try to rush yourself. Respect your own needs. For instance, if it takes more than two weeks to master PSR using the full-length instructions, take the time you need before going on to the abbreviated version. Similarly, if you find that it takes you more than five minutes to relax using the short form of PSR, take all the time you need.

Years of experience demonstrates that a month is the minimum amount of time required to fully master PSR; yet benefits will start accruing immediately after you start.

One final point: even after you've graduated to the abbreviated form of PSR, it is advisable to return to the full-length instructions once every month or so. This helps keep you "on track" and ensures that you're performing the exercise correctly.

Here are two scripts, both adapted from Spencer A. Rathus and Jeffrey S. Nevid in their book, *BT: Behavior Therapy: Strategies for Solving Problems in Living.*

Full-length PSR Instructions

Settle back and find a comfortable position. Make sure that all your clothing is loose. Move your head around a little, getting it comfortably settled. Get your legs into a comfortable position also. Do the same with your arms. Take a comfortable, deep breath and hold it for six or seven seconds. Let it out slowly, relaxing while you do so. Close your eyes.

Focus your attention on your hands. Clench them tightly, making a fist. Hold them that way for six or seven seconds. One, two, three, four, five, six, seven. Feel the pressure. Now just let them go. Feel the difference in the feelings. When your fists were clenched, there was tension. When you let them go, the muscles began to feel relaxed and loose. Study the difference. For about fifteen seconds, allow the relaxed feeling to develop and swell. Feel your hands become comfortably relaxed and loose. [Maintain approximately fifteen seconds of silence.] (Note: throughout this exercise, allow about fifteen seconds to let the feelings of relaxation develop and swell following each instruction to relax.) Now clench your fists again for several seconds and study the tension. One, two, three, four, five, six, seven. Now relax them. Study the contrast between tension and relaxation. Let the feeling grow. [Maintain approximately fifteen seconds of silence.]

Now focus on your biceps. Allowing your hands to remain relaxed, bend your arms at the elbows and tense your biceps. Hold the tension. One, two, three, four, five, six, seven. Now relax your biceps. Just let your arms go limp. Feel the difference. Be aware of the warm feeling in your hands flowing up through your arms. This is relaxation. Let the warm, comfortable feeling swell and develop. [Maintain approximately fifteen seconds of silence.] Now bend your elbows and tense your biceps again, studying the tension. One, two, three, four, five, six, seven. Now relax. Let the tension go. Feel the warm current of relaxation flow through your hands and arms. Allow this feeling to grow. [Maintain approximately fifteen seconds of silence.]

Focus on your triceps. Tense your triceps, and feel the tension along the back of your arms. Hold it. One, two, three, four, five, six, seven. Now relax. Let all the tension go. Let go of all contractions anywhere in your arms. Allow them to go limp. Allow the warm current of relaxation to flow through your arms. [Maintain approximately fifteen seconds of silence.]

Now tighten your triceps again and feel the tension. Hold. One, two, three, four, five, six, seven. And now relax. Note the warmth flowing through your arms. Let your arms become heavier. Feel the relaxation throughout your arms. [Maintain approximately fifteen seconds of silence.]

Allow your arms to remain comfortably relaxed, and focus on your forehead. Tense your forehead by frowning, and study the tension as you do so. Hold it. One, two, three, four, five, six, seven. Now let the tension go. Picture your forehead becoming very smooth, and allow the feelings of relaxation to spread across your forehead and your scalp. [Maintain approximately fifteen seconds of silence.] Now scrunch up your forehead again.

Feel the knotted, tight muscles. Hold it. One, two, three, four, five, six, seven. Relax. Feel the tension ease. Allow that comfortable feeling of relaxation to permeate your forehead and flow across your scalp. [Maintain approximately fifteen seconds of silence.]

Now focus on the central area of your face. Tense up your nasal area. Feel the tension. Hold it. One, two, three, four, five, six, seven. Now relax. Allow the relaxed feeling to flow from your forehead to the central area of your face and back again. Let it spread to your scalp. Enjoy the absence of tension. [Maintain approximately fifteen seconds of silence.] Now tense your nasal area again. Tighten it. Hold. One, two, three, four, five, six, seven. Now let it go. Feel the difference between tension and relaxation. Just let the feeling grow and spread across your face. [Maintain approximately fifteen seconds of silence.]

Now focus on your mouth. Keeping the rest of your face as relaxed as possible, press your lips together hard and study the tension as you do so. Hold it. One, two, three, four, five, six, seven. Now let the tension go. Part your lips slightly and let all the tension in your face go. Feel the relaxed feeling grow. [Maintain approximately fifteen seconds of silence.] Now press your lips together again. Press. Hold. One, two, three, four, five, six, seven. Now let them go. Part them comfortably, and note the warm, pleasant feeling of relaxation. Allow it to spread into the nasal region and up to your forehead and scalp. Feel the loose, comfortable feeling. [Maintain approximately fifteen seconds of silence.]

Allow your arms and face to remain relaxed. Focus on your neck, tensing the muscles there. Study the tension. Hold. One, two, three, four, five, six, seven. Now let the contraction go. Relax your neck area completely. Allow the warm current of relaxation to flow down from your forehead, through your nasal and mouth areas, and into your neck. Feel the difference between tension and relaxation. Let the feeling of relaxation grow. [Maintain approximately fifteen seconds of silence.] Now tense your neck again. Tighten the muscles. Tighten. One, two, three, four, five, six, seven. Now let it all go. Feel the difference. Permit your head and neck to relax completely, and feel the warmth. [Maintain approximately fifteen seconds of silence.]

Allowing your neck to remain relaxed, focus on your shoulders. Tense your shoulder muscles and feel the tension. Hold. One, two, three, four, five, six, seven. Now let the tension go and allow your shoulders to relax completely. Feel the difference. Allow the relaxation to flow from your head and neck to your shoulders. Let the feeling swell and grow. [Maintain approximately fifteen seconds of silence.] Now tense your shoulders again. Really tighten them. Tight. Hold. One, two, three, four, five, six, seven. Now release the tension completely. Imagine that your shoulders are limp and heavy. Feel the relaxation. Allow this natural feeling of relaxation to spread throughout your shoulders, neck, face, and scalp. [Maintain approximately fifteen seconds of silence.]

Now concentrate on your stomach. Permitting the rest of your body to remain relaxed, draw your stomach in. Breathe deeply and hold. Feel the tension. Hold it. One, two, three, four, five, six, seven. Now exhale and let go of your contraction simultaneously. Note the difference in the feelings. Allow your stomach to relax completely. Breathe comfortably and let the warm feeling of relaxation spread throughout your stomach region. [Maintain approximately fifteen seconds of silence.] Again, take in a deep breath and suck in your stomach hard. Tighten. Hold. One, two, three, four, five, six, seven. Now let out your breath and relax your stomach muscles at the same moment. Feel the contrast. Feel the comfort of relaxation. Continue to breathe comfortably, easily, and regularly. Allow the relaxation to develop on its own. [Maintain approximately fifteen seconds of silence.]

Turn your attention to your buttocks. Tighten your buttocks. Hold. One, two, three, four, five, six, seven. Now release the tension, permitting your buttocks to relax completely. Feel the relaxation. Allow it to spread throughout the buttocks and abdominal region. Enjoy the pleasant sensations. [Maintain approximately fifteen seconds of silence.] Now tighten your buttocks again, tight. Hold it. One, two, three, four, five, six, seven. Now let the tension go. Relax all the muscles and feel the sharp contrast. Allow the relaxation to swell and develop. Breathe comfortably. [Maintain approximately fifteen seconds of silence.]

Now focus on the muscles in your thighs. Breathe in deeply and tighten these muscles. Hold the tension. One, two, three, four, five, six, seven. Now tell yourself to relax; exhale, and release the tension in your thighs completely. Allow them to become limp as you breathe gently and regularly. Feel the comfortable feeling of relaxation. Allow it to grow. [Maintain approximately fifteen seconds of silence.] Now inhale deeply and tense your thigh muscles again. Tighten them. Hold. One, two, three, four, five, six, seven. Now let out your breath and let all the tension go. Allow the feeling of warmth to spread throughout your thighs. [Maintain approximately fifteen seconds of silence.]

Maintaining the relaxation in your thighs, focus on your calves. Take a deep breath and tighten your calf muscles. Hold. One, two, three, four, five, six, seven. Now tell yourself to relax and just let go of your breath and your muscles. Study the contrast in your feelings. Allow the warm current of relaxation to flow from your thighs to your calves. Your legs are feeling heavy and limp. Enjoy the comfortable feeling of relaxation. [Maintain approximately fifteen seconds of silence.] Now breathe in again, and tighten the muscles of your calves. Hold it. One, two, three, four, five, six, seven. Now let your breath go and allow your calf muscles to relax completely. Once again, feel the warmth spread throughout your legs. Allow them to go limp. [Maintain approximately fifteen seconds of silence.]

Now focus on your feet. Keeping your thighs and calves as relaxed as possible, take in a deep breath and clench your toes like a fist. Hold them that way and study the tension. Hold. One, two, three, four, five, six, seven. Now simultaneously release your breath and your toes. Allow your feet to relax and feel the difference. Breathe comfortably, and let the relaxation move from your upper legs, into your calves, and then into your feet. Allow the warmth and comfort to grow. [Maintain approximately fifteen seconds of silence.] Now once again, breathe in deeply and tighten your feet. Feel the tight muscles. Hold it.

One, two, three, four, five, six, seven. Now exhale and relax your feet completely. Feel the warm current of relaxation flow throughout both your legs. Enjoy the sensation. [Maintain approximately fifteen seconds of silence.]

Sit or lie comfortably, allowing your entire body to delight in the feeling of relaxation. Now go back and check for any little pockets of tension. Take a comfortable breath. Focus on your hands and arms, and release any tension there, allowing them to relax even further. Now focus on your face. Picture your forehead smooth and relaxed. Relax your mouth area, parting your lips slightly. Focus on your shoulders and neck. Release any tension you feel there, allowing them to become even looser. Release any tension in your abdomen and buttocks. Allow your legs and feet to go limp. Sense the warm current flowing throughout your body. Sense how heavy and comfortable your limbs and body feel.

Continue relaxing like that, enjoying the feelings of warmth and comfort. Breathe comfortably, and with each exhalation, tell yourself to relax more.

When you are ready, open your eyes. Stretch comfortably. Get up slowly and move about slowly at first, since your muscle tone has decreased and it will take a few moments for it to return to normal.

Abbreviated PSR Instructions

Settle back comfortably. Make sure that all your clothing is loose. Take a few comfortable, deep breaths. Stretch gently. Take another deep breath and let it out all at once. Close your eyes.

Focus on your arms. Take a breath, hold it, and tighten the muscles in your hands and arms. Hold the tension. One, two, three, four, five, six, seven. Now tell yourself to relax. Release your breath and let go of the tension in your hands and arms. Feel the difference between the tension and the relaxation. Allow the warm current of relaxation to flow through your hands and arms. Allow it to swell and develop. [Maintain approximately fifteen seconds of silence.] Now breathe in again. Hold it, and tighten the muscles in your hands and arms. Tighten. Hold. One, two, three, four, five, six, seven. Now all at once, release your breath and relax the contractions in your hands and arms. Study the feeling of relaxation. Breathe gently and comfortably as you allow it to flow up and down both arms. [Maintain approximately fifteen seconds of silence.]

Keeping your arms relaxed, focus your attention on your face. Take a deep breath and scrunch up your forehead and nose, while you press your lips together. Press. Hold the tension. Hold. One, two, three, four, five, six, seven. Simultaneously release your breath and let go of all the tension in your face. Relax all the muscles, and part your lips slightly. Allow all the tension to disappear. Feel the warmth flowing into your forehead and scalp. Allow the relaxation to develop. [Maintain approximately fifteen seconds of silence.] Now breathe in deeply and tighten all the muscles of your face again. Tighten.

Hold it. One, two, three, four, five, six, seven. Exhale and relax. Allow the relaxation to develop. Picture your forehead, and all the muscles of your face, as smooth and relaxed. [Maintain approximately fifteen seconds of silence.]

Now focus your attention on your neck, shoulders, abdomen, and buttocks. Take a deep breath and tighten all these muscle groups. Contract all the muscles of your trunk. Tighten. Hold. One, two, three, four, five, six, seven. Let your breath out all at once and simultaneously release all the tension throughout your central region. Allow all the muscles to relax. Study the contrast between tension and relaxation. Allow the warm current of relaxation to flow down from your face and throughout your neck...shoulders...abdomen...and buttocks. Once again, breathe deeply and tighten all these muscles. Study the tension. Hold. One, two, three, four, five, six, seven. Now tell yourself to relax, and let go of all the contractions at once. Feel the relaxation and comfort. Just let it flow and develop. [Maintain approximately fifteen seconds of silence.]

Now attend to your legs and feet. Keeping the rest of your body relaxed, take a deep breath and tighten the muscles of your legs and feet. Study the tension from your thighs, through your calves, and into your ankles and toes. Hold it. One, two, three, four, five, six, seven. Release your breath and relax all the contractions in your legs and feet. Breathe comfortably as you feel the absence of tension. Your legs feel heavy and limp. Allow the relaxation to develop. [Maintain approximately fifteen seconds of silence.] Okay. Once again: Breathe in. Tighten your leg muscles, clench your toes into a fist. Hold. One, two, three, four, five, six, seven. All at once, exhale and release the tension. Breathe gently, easily, and regularly, and feel the relaxation travel from your hands and arms, across your face, through your neck and shoulders, and through your abdomen and buttocks, into your legs and feet. Enjoy the sensation of the warmth moving throughout your body. Notice how much you relax with each exhalation. Continue allowing these feelings of relaxation to develop on their own. [Maintain approximately fifteen seconds of silence.]

When you're ready, open your eyes. Stretch gently. Slowly get up, giving yourself plenty of time to adjust to moving about.

Relaxation Methods Two and Three: The Empty Movie Theatre and Sensory Fantasy

The following two relaxation methods are best learned after you've learned PSR and have become familiar with the feeling of deep relaxation. These methods are not substitutes for PSR, but alternatives to be used after you've practiced both the long and the short form of PSR for at least two weeks.

Relaxation Method Two: The Empty Movie Theatre

Choose a quiet time, and find a place that will be free of distractions for at least 15 minutes. Sit comfortably or stretch out on a bed or couch. Loosen clothing. Close your eyes, and begin breathing deeply and comfortably. Do not force, but allow your breath to penetrate deep into your lungs.

Here are two tests that will tell you whether you're breathing correctly:

- You should feel the waistband on your slacks or skirt tighten slightly on each inhalation; when you exhale, the feeling of tightness should disappear.

- Place your right hand on your chest and your left hand on your abdomen. When you breathe, your right hand should not move at all. Your left hand should be lifted by your abdomen when you breathe in, as your abdominal cavity expands; your left hand should fall as you exhale.

Continue breathing deeply, and as you do so, imagine yourself sitting in the center of a totally dark theatre. You are alone. An enormous screen stretches across the front of the theatre. It is entirely dark, except for one thing: in the center of the screen, there is one tiny pinhole of light. It is the only light you can see. Focus on that light. Think of nothing else.

As you continue to focus on the tiny dot of light, allow your body to relax. Imagine yourself sinking more deeply into the chair, bed, or couch. Feel it enveloping you. Imagine that your body is becoming increasingly limp. Remind yourself that you are feeling safe, comfortable, and relaxed.

Maintain this activity for fifteen minutes. If thoughts intrude in your mind, don't fight them or try to push them away; just let them go. Imagine that they are like motes of dust caught in the beam of light. You just watch them come and go. Do the same with any environmental distractions. For example, if a door closes in a room nearby, just acknowledge the noise and let it go.

After fifteen minutes, slowly return to the present. Give yourself a few moments to adjust to your actual surroundings.

When you have done this exercise several times, you will be able to achieve a remarkable degree of relaxation with near-perfect reliability.

Relaxation Method Three: Sensory Fantasy

This is very similar to the Empty Movie Theatre method, but it involves picturing a more detailed relaxing scene. Prepare yourself in the same way: choose a quiet, distraction-free environment. Sit or lie comfortably. Loosen clothing. Close your eyes. Breathe deeply.

For this technique, conjure up a particularly pleasant and soothing memory — a special place that was particularly relaxing for you. You might imagine yourself at the seashore, sitting in a comfortable lounge chair, looking out over a sandy beach toward the ocean. The bright sun warms your skin. You can smell the ocean, hear the surging background noises of the surf and gulls as they circle and dive. You can see the sun glinting off the water and, in the distance, two boats with cool white sails.

Or you might recall lying on a blanket at a picnic. You are flat on your back, staring up at a deep blue sky. A few white clouds drift by slowly. You can hear the sound of birds singing in nearby trees. The smell of newly mown grass is in the air. A soft breeze caresses your skin.

As these descriptions suggest, vivid, sensory memories are at the heart of this method. It's not enough to recall a pleasant place in general. Instead, recall specific sense memories: What do you see? What do you feel on your skin or under your body? What sounds to you hear? What odors can you detect? The more vivid the sense memories, the more engrossing and relaxing the sensory fantasy.

Visit your special relaxing place for fifteen minutes, then slowly return to the present. Give yourself a few moments to adjust to your actual surroundings.

This technique, practiced faithfully, provides a highly reliable and effective way of achieving a state of relaxation.

Once you can relax at will, you can make excellent use of the technique of desensitization.

How To Desensitize Yourself

First, clearly define the "target situation," the one you avoid. For example, if you're reluctant to look for a new job because you're afraid of being interviewed, your target situation is "sitting with an interviewer, being interviewed for a job."

Once you have your target situation clearly in mind, you can desensitize yourself by imagining your way through a series of steps of graduated difficulty, each more closely approaching the situation you fear. Sometimes you can use photos or other aids. At every step, relaxation techniques help you tolerate whatever is fearful for you at that stage. When you can imagine yourself in that frightening situation while remaining completely relaxed for several minutes — and when you can do this three consecutive times — you can then move on to the next step. Ultimately, you will be able to remain completely relaxed as you picture yourself in the target situation.

Desensitization can rarely be done in one sitting, or even in a few. The actual length of time it takes varies according to these factors:

- The intensity of the fear you experience when you imagine yourself in the target situation.

- The number of steps in the hierarchy you construct (these are determined by the nature and complexity of the target situation). Remember, you can't rush this process. Each step in your hierarchy should be only slightly more unsettling than the one before. You must be completely desensitized to each step before you can proceed.

- The length of time it takes you to reach the goal of three successive exposures lasting several minutes each, during which you remain completely relaxed. This may take up to 20 exposures.

Since no desensitization session should last longer than an hour, and since several sessions may be required to overcome your fear, you may need a considerable length of time to complete a desensitization program. Nevertheless, the time will have been well spent, since the effectiveness of this technique has repeatedly been demonstrated.

Using the employment interview situation as an example, here are the specifics of what you would do next. To construct your own hierarchy, you will need a set of 3 by 5 cards.

First, list the incremental steps leading up to your target situation. Use one 3 by 5 card per instruction:

1. I'm leaving home for the interview.

2. I'm arriving at the office building where the interview will be conducted.

3. I'm entering the building.

4. I'm standing in the lobby, studying the building directory to figure out where the interviewer's office is.

5. I'm approaching the elevator.

6. I'm waiting for the elevator.

7. I'm getting on the elevator.

8. I'm taking the elevator to the correct floor.

9. I'm walking down the corridor toward the office.

10. I'm entering the office.

11. I'm introducing myself to the receptionist.

12. I'm waiting for the interviewer to invite me into his or her office.

Next, number the cards, using 1 for the least frightening step and ending with the target situation. Arrange the cards in increasing order, from the least to the most frightening scenario.

If you want to use aids to make your fantasies as realistic as possible, do so. In this case, for example, you might plan to dress for each desensitization session in the clothing you'd wear for the interview.

In other cases, make use of photographs or other items. One swimmer who was afraid of diving into a swimming pool applied suntan lotion before beginning his sessions to conjure up some of the sensations he might experience at poolside.

Begin each desensitization session by relaxing, using the abbreviated form of PSR or one of the other relaxation techniques just described.

When you're relaxed, read the first card in your numbered series. Vividly imagine the situation you've written on the card. Use the theatre of the mind to construct a detailed, lifelike scene. Use all your senses.

- See yourself in the situation (picture the office building, the doors through which you enter, the lobby, the potted plants, the security guard, the elevator, and so on).

- Hear the sounds you might hear if you were actually there (conjure up typical office building sounds, such as telephones ringing, elevator doors opening and closing, computer monitors humming, the whine of dot-matrix printers, murmured conversations).

- Feel the sensations (feel the carpet beneath your shoes, the lack of fresh air, the sense of being inside an ascending elevator, the feelings of the vinyl upholstery in the waiting room).

- Smell the odors (smell the glue from new carpets, the faint odor of cigarettes, the perfumes worn by the women employees, the smell of coffee and doughnuts).

Hold this vivid scene in your mind until you begin to feel frightened. Then stop your imagining. Either make your mind go blank or picture the peaceful, relaxing scene you created for the third relaxation method, the sensory fantasy. Practice your relaxation technique until your fear is replaced by a feeling of calmness. This may take anywhere from two to ten minutes. (If you cannot achieve calmness after ten minutes, try repeating the prior scene in your hierarchy of fearful situations, or create an incremental middle step that you can handle.)

Imagine the same feared situation again. You'll be able to keep it in mind longer now. When it becomes uncomfortable for you, put the scene out of your mind and relax yourself again. Repeat this procedure until the situation no longer evokes fear.

When you can think about the situation three consecutive times (for several minutes each time) without feeling any fear, move on to the next card in the series and repeat the process. (There is no hard-and-fast rule about how many exposures are required before the three-times-without-fear effect occurs. Sometimes ten or twenty exposures are necessary. Other times, only two or three will suffice. Take the time you need!) Continue on through the entire series of cards. In the end, you will be able to contemplate the target situation while remaining totally relaxed.

After you've properly completed the procedure, you'll be able to approach the actual situation fearlessly. Fear will no longer prevent you from taking important risks.

Examples for You To Try

In each case that follows, you are presented with a risk-inhibiting fear that can be overcome by means of the desensitization method. Using as guides the examples and instructions above, identify the target situation and construct a hierarchy of steps that might be used by a person wishing to overcome the fear. Write as though you were the person, using the first-person pronoun, *I*. Twelve blanks are provided in each example, but you can construct a hierarchy with more or fewer steps (use extra paper if you need it). Sample answers appear after each example.

Case One: The Swimmer

David is a 43-year-old man who has recently learned to swim. He wants to learn to dive from a diving board, but is afraid to.

Target Situation:

Steps:

1. _____
2. _____
3. _____
4. _____
5. _____
6. _____
7. _____
8. _____
9. _____
10. _____
11. _____
12. _____

Sample Answers

Target Situation: Diving into a swimming pool from a diving board.

Steps:

1. I'm arriving at the pool. The sun is hot. I'm standing by the entrance gate, watching the people swim. I hear the voices, the splashes of the divers. I can smell suntan lotion and chlorine.

2. I've found a place to sit. I'm stripping down to my suit and settling into the lounge chair.

3. I'm getting up from the chair and walking toward the diving board.

4. I'm standing at the diving board, watching other people dive into the water.

5. I'm stepping up onto the diving board.

6. I'm walking along the diving board.

7. I'm standing at the end of the diving board.

8. I'm falling forward from the diving board into the water.

Case Two: The Musician

Jill is an accomplished pianist who has never played for anyone other than family members and a few close friends. She's been asked by a friend to play at a fund-raiser for a local charity. She would like to oblige, since she believes in the cause, but is terrified at the prospect of performing in front of an audience of nearly 200 people.

Target Situation:

Steps:

1. _____
2. _____
3. _____
4. _____
5. _____
6. _____
7. _____
8. _____
9. _____
10. _____
11. _____

12. _____

Sample Answers

Target Situation: Sitting confidently at the piano on the day of the fund-raiser, just about to begin playing.

Steps:

1. I'm getting dressed for the concert; I brush my clothes and look in the mirror, combing my hair.

2. I'm collecting the music I'll bring with me.

3. I'm putting the music in my car. I hear the car door slam shut.

4. I'm getting into the car. I can smell the upholstery.

5. I'm starting the engine.

6. I'm driving to the fund-raiser. I note landmarks as I get closer and closer.

7. I'm arriving at the fund-raiser. There are lots of other cars there belonging to people who will be in the audience. They're all dressed up.

8. I'm walking into the building. I can hear my footsteps echoing in the hallway.

9. I'm speaking with my friend as she shows me to the piano. I can smell the polish that was used to wax the piano. I can see my reflection in its surface.

10. I'm placing my music on the piano.

11. I'm waiting off-stage as my friend introduces me to the audience.

12. I'm walking onto the stage and sitting at the piano.

Using Desensitization To Overcome Your Own Fears

Now return to your Personal Risk Agenda (from Chapter 3) and Personal Fear Profile (from Chapter 4). Select a risk that you've been avoiding. Identify your own target situation and set up a desensitization hierarchy that will enable you to take the risk you want without fear.

Target Situation:

Steps:

1. _____

2. _____

3. _____

4. _____

5. _____

6. _____

7. _____

8. _____

9. _____

10. _____

11. _____

12. _____

Do the same with as many risks as you wish. Use a blank sheet of paper for each fear to construct a target situation and a hierarchy.

Over the next several weeks, master the relaxation exercises above. Then choose one of the risks for which you've set up a hierarchy. Use the desensitization technique to banish your fear.

If you need training to carry off your project skillfully, get it. For example, if you're afraid of striking up a conversation with attractive members of the opposite sex because you fear that you'll be unable to maintain a conversation, then take a course in interpersonal communication to build your conversational skills.

Also remember to rehearse. If the target situation requires interacting with other people — as in the case of the job interview — have a friend or family member role-play the scene with you. Similarly, if you have to give a talk, rehearse it. These strategies provide halfway points between vivid imagining and the actual situation you fear.

Technique Two: The Threshold Method

The threshold method is most useful when the target situation is one you can gradually approach in actuality without undue inconvenience or hardship. You can use it instead of desensitization when you can control your fear and regain composure simply by remaining in the situation for a reasonable length of time. The method is different from desensitization in that it is not a mental exercise; but it's similar in that it makes use of a series of graduated steps, each of which brings you closer to your target situation.

As you arrive at each step, you can expect to feel uneasy at first. As with the desensitization process, you remain in the situation until you've calmed down. After your uneasiness disappears, you then proceed to the next step. Once again, you will feel uneasy. Stay there until you achieve a state of calmness again. Continue through the entire series of graduated steps until you reach your target situation.

For example, suppose your fear of disapproval prevents you from openly stating your views on a controversial topic. Perhaps you believe in a woman's right to abortion, but feel afraid of expressing your opinion to a parent or friend.

Using the threshold method, here's what you'd do.

First, you'd identify your target situation. In this case, it's taking the self-disclosure risk of expressing your opinion about abortion to a person whose disapproval you fear.

Next, you'd create a set of graduated steps leading up to that situation. Beginning with a step that's only a little fear-inducing, you'd proceed through a series of measures, each one slightly more threatening than the one before.

Here's what a series of graduated steps might look like:

1. Talk with the person about a subject *other* than the controversial one.

2. Talk with the person about subjects related to the controversial topic (for example, unwanted children).

3. Talk with the person about the subject of abortion, but offer no opinion.

4. Talk with the person about the controversial topic without offering your own opinion, but do so in the presence of someone who shares your view and is willing to express it. Do not indicate agreement with the point of view your ally expresses.

5. Talk with the person again about the controversial topic without offering your own opinion. Do it in the presence of someone who expresses your view. Indicate agreement when your ally expresses the opinion you share. You may do so non-verbally (by nodding, for example), or by reinforcing the message (by saying "Yes!" or "That's a good point!").

6. Talk with the person in the presence of a supporter, and openly express your views about the controversial topic.

7. Talk with the person alone, and openly express your views about the controversial topic.

The number of graduated steps you formulate may be more or fewer than seven. For example, you might talk with the person many times, gradually revealing more and more of your opinion, thereby increasing the number of steps in the program you design.

The steps you formulate can be different from those suggested here. For example, your steps might involve use of the telephone (since you may find it safer to risk disapproval when speaking on the phone rather than in person).

The only hard-and-fast rule about a threshold hierarchy is that the number of steps should be determined after careful analysis of the feared situation and the degree of fear evoked by each step. Every step in the hierarchy must be only slightly more frightening then the one before. However, there are a few key principles that govern the use of the threshold method.

Keys to the Threshold Method

First, your progress should be incremental. In other words, don't expect rapid progress; rather, slow, steady movement is what you're after.

Second, work with each step until you no longer feel *any* discomfort in that situation. Don't rationalize your feelings of discomfort or skip any steps in your urgency to move ahead.

The threshold method helps you ease into a situation you fear. In the example above, you prepare yourself for the sting of disapproval, just as you might prepare yourself to get a shot (if you were afraid of getting shots). You also take some of the poison out of the sting by revealing your position gradually.

The third key principle is that where other people are involved, it's best to anticipate their reaction as much as you can. Prepare rejoinders to use if you are criticized. Or prepare a silent message for yourself that will help you stick to your guns and stay cool. An example of such a message is, "I have a right to my opinion, and I don't have to feel bad because this person disagrees with me."

Example

Mike, an athletic 28-year-old, was a good intermediate tennis player. Although he loved to play, he had never signed up for a tournament for fear of losing and feeling embarrassed. He knew that playing in tournaments would be a good way to sharpen his competitive skills and meet new tennis partners. His avoidance of competitions frustrated and annoyed him. He set up this series of steps to overcome his fear:

1. Begin by attending two small, local tournaments as an observer. (My local tennis club will be able to tell me where and when they'll be held.) As I watch, imagine how it might feel to be in each player's shoes. Remind myself that feelings about competition are largely a matter of what an individual competitor brings to the game.

2. While watching the second tournament, pick a person who seems to have a good attitude toward competition — someone who seems to really delight in playing,

but at the same time plays aggressively. Make it a point to talk with that competitor about his or her attitude toward competition.

3. Sign up for a tournament for players at my level, to be held several months in the future, at a club that's not far from home.

4. Visit the courts several weeks ahead of time. Walk around them, and become familiar with the facility, visiting the locker room and the lounge.

5. Following my first visit to the facility, rent a court for an hour, bring along a nonthreatening partner, and do some light hitting.

6. Visit the courts again. This time, bring a tough partner and play competitively. As I play, work on becoming accustomed to the setting, sounds, and sights of the facility.

7. Repeat step six once more, adding an incentive for the winner. (The loser will buy lunch.)

8. Ask the manager of my local tennis club for the name of someone — a stranger — who plays at my level. Phone this person and repeat steps six and seven.

9. On the day of the tournament, arrive early, become acclimated to the facility once again, and let the tournament organizers know that I'm ready to play.

By following this series of steps, Mike gradually overcame his reluctance to play in tournaments.

Action Steps

The threshold method works for all the fears listed in Chapter 4. Follow these instructions:

1. Review your Personal Risk Inventory (see Chapter 3) and identify a risk you want to take but haven't.

2. Select some specific situation in which it would be possible for you to take the risk. (Don't do this exercise in the abstract; you must have in mind an actual, feasible risk.)

3. Construct a series of graduated steps that approach the target situation (the risk you've identified in instruction 1). Compose your hierarchy in the first person, using the present imperative mode ("Find the customer service area.").

4. Compare your graduated steps for each fear with those outlined in the examples in this chapter. Remember, each step should be only slightly more fear-inducing than the preceding step.

5. Slowly proceed from each step to the next. Do not move ahead until you can comfortably remain on the step you've reached. Do not skip any steps.

6. Continue through all the steps until you reach the target situation.

Examples for You To Try

In each case that follows, you are presented with a fear that can be overcome by means of the threshold method. Use the example and instructions above as guidelines. Identify the target situation and construct a hierarchy of steps that might be used by a person wishing to overcome the fear. Write as though you were that person, using the first person pronoun *I*. Create between seven and twelve steps for your hierarchy. Sample answers follow each case.

Case One: The Young Shopper

Marie, a 16-year-old, bought her prom dress in a large department store a few weeks ago. After trying it on again at home, she decided to return it. She's never returned an item before. Unfortunately, she's misplaced the receipt. The store has a strict policy: "No refunds without receipt."

Target Situation:

Steps:

1. _____
2. _____
3. _____
4. _____
5. _____
6. _____
7. _____
8. _____
9. _____
10. _____

11. _____

12. _____

Sample Answers

Target Situation: Standing at the customer service desk and negotiating the return of the prom dress without a receipt.

Steps:

1. Visit the store where I bought the dress. Walk around until I feel comfortable in the store.

2. During my next visit, find the customer service area. From a distance, observe the general workings of the department.

3. During my third visit, return to the customer service desk. Stand close enough so that I can watch and listen as other people transact business there.

4. On my fourth visit, step up to the counter. Ask questions about the store's return policy (or some other topic) in a nonchallenging way. Do not mention my problem.

5. Visit the customer service desk again. This time, ask about exceptions to the store's policy about returning an item without a receipt. Get the names of managers who have the authority to give me my money back under these circumstances. Find what supporting materials I might need.

6. Prepare myself carefully. Gather all the necessary documentation (such as a canceled check or credit card records). Formulate at least one or two alternative solutions that would satisfy me, even though they might not be exactly what I hope for — for example, a store credit. Anticipate the arguments I am likely to hear and prepare responses. Prepare worst-contingency responses, such as threatening to hire a lawyer or calling the Better Business Bureau.

7. Go to the customer service counter and try to return the item for a refund.

Case Two: Sam

Sam is a 23-year-old man who has a fear of sharing personal information about himself with members of the opposite sex. (Personal information includes statements about who you are; where you come from; what your values are; what pleases, angers, saddens, and confuses you; what your family is like; and what you hope for in life.) Sam realizes that to build and maintain a close and honest relationship, it's necessary to reveal some personal information to his partner. His history includes a number of relationships, all of which have failed. Some simply petered out when Sam wouldn't open up. Others ended when Sam bolted because of his discomfort at having revealed too much personal information.

Target Situation:

Steps:

1. _____
2. _____
3. _____
4. _____
5. _____
6. _____
7. _____
8. _____
9. _____
10. _____
11. _____
12. _____

Sample Answers

Target Situation: Being in the company of a woman and revealing appropriate personal information.

Steps:

1. List several facts about myself that are unknown to my companion.

2. Rank these facts according to how difficult they are for me to reveal. They should range from the impersonal and nonthreatening ("I was born in Illinois," "I work as a bank teller") through the moderately personal and threatening ("my parents practiced different religions," "I'm attending college at night"), to quite personal and threatening revelations ("my father was an alcoholic," "I'm divorced and have a child"). List at least five or six facts at each level of difficulty. I will keep in mind the appropriateness of the information I reveal in terms of the intimacy of my relationship with this person.

3. In the course of one conversation, share an impersonal and nonthreatening revelation.

4. After I feel comfortable about having accomplished step 3, reveal another fact of about equal difficulty.

5. Continue revealing "safe" facts until I can remain very relaxed during and after the conversation.

6. In a later conversation, share some slightly more personal fact — one I feel only slightly uncomfortable revealing.

7. After I feel relaxed with step 6, select another fact that is just about as difficult to reveal. Continue revealing facts at that level of difficulty until I can remain very relaxed during and after the conversation.

8. Continue revealing moderately threatening personal information in the course of several conversations until I can do so without experiencing discomfort.

9. Select a revelation that is rather threatening (but appropriate to my degree of intimacy with my companion). After having revealed moderately threatening personal information during other conversations (and remaining relaxed), disclose this more difficult piece of information.

Using the Threshold Method to Overcome Your Own Fears

Now return to your Personal Risk Agenda (in Chapter 3), and your Personal Fear Profile (in Chapter 4). Select a risk you've been avoiding. Identify your target situation and set up a threshold hierarchy that will enable you to approach the target gradually.

Target Situation:

Steps:

1. _____

2. _____

3. _____

4. _____

5. _____

6. _____

7. _____

8. _____

9. _____

10. _____

11. _____

12. _____

Repeat this with as many risks as you wish. (Use a blank sheet of paper to construct a target situation and a hierarchy for each fear.)

When you're ready, follow the threshold method instructions to overcome your fear of taking each risk.

The two behavioral techniques described in this chapter are highly effective. An additional and equally effective set of techniques is described in the next chapter.

Further Reading

Rathus, S.A., and J.S. Nevid. (1977) *BT: Behavior Therapy: Strategies for Solving Problems in Living*. New York: Signet Books.

6

Overcoming Your Fear of Risk-Taking by Changing the Way You Think

Cognitive Techniques for Change

The threshold method and systematic desensitization work by replacing fear with calmness. They don't require paying attention to the thoughts that give rise to your fears. By contrast, the techniques described in this chapter help you eliminate fear by challenging the irrational beliefs and logical distortions that create it.

Cognitive techniques are based on common sense. They require no special expertise or sophisticated understanding of human psychology. Most people can easily learn how to use these techniques, and they often work relatively quickly. By applying them properly and conscientiously, you can anticipate good success in overcoming your fears.

Cognitive techniques rest on three key ideas:

1. The way you think influences the way you feel and behave. Distorted thinking leads to erroneous conclusions and inappropriate, invariably negative, feelings. These, in turn, lead to self-defeating, self-limiting, or overly cautious behavior. For example, an older person who constantly tells himself, "I'll make a fool of myself if I try to learn to play the piano at my age" will probably avoid doing it.

2. You cannot change reality, but you can change the way you think about it. For example, you can't make someone like you if he or she doesn't; but you can remind yourself that your happiness and sense of self-worth don't depend on your popularity with one particular person. Similarly, you can't remove the element of risk from asking someone out on a date, but you can reassure yourself that it isn't essential to your survival or self-esteem that your invitation be accepted.

3. Events alone can't cause you to experience negative emotions such as fear, depression, and loneliness. The combination of events *plus* the way you think about them is what determines your feelings and behavior. By changing the way you think about events, you can change the way you feel and behave.

The Relationship Between Events, Thoughts, and Feelings

This point is critical: events alone can't cause you to experience negative emotions. Your understanding of this will lay the groundwork for learning the cognitive techniques in this chapter.

The diagram below depicts the way most people see the relationship between events (A) and feelings (C).

Events (A)   ————————————————————→   Feelings (C)

The solid line indicates a direct cause-and-effect relationship between the two: you probably believe that events cause your feelings. For example, suppose your car breaks down on the way to a very important job interview. (The car's breakdown under these circumstances is an "event.") You feel wildly frustrated and upset. At that moment, if someone were to ask you why you're upset, you'd probably say, "because my car broke down." Your words reveal your belief that your feelings were caused by the car's breakdown. The situation is shown below.

Events (A)   ————————————————————→   Feelings (C)

Car breaks down on the way   You feel frustrated
to an important interview   and upset

But if you didn't care about making the interview, would you feel so frustrated and upset? Probably not. Most likely you'd just feel annoyed about the inconvenience of having to deal with a malfunctioning car. It isn't really the breakdown itself that causes your feelings to surge. It's the breakdown *plus* your expectations about the interview.

It's inaccurate to blame events for the way you feel. Events contribute to your feelings. But your own internal thoughts play a crucial role as well (for example, your thought might have been, "My future success depends on getting to the interview on time.") Change your thoughts, and you can change your response to events.

Believing otherwise suggests that your feelings are nothing more than automatic, objective responses to the things that happen to you. It implies that you have no *control* over how you feel. If good things happen to you, you feel good. If bad things happen to you, you feel bad.

Such a view doesn't account for those instances in which bad things happen to people but they rise above them, or use them somehow to turn bad into good. You're laid off from a job you've held for ten years; but instead of feeling overwhelmed by depression and a sense of unfairness, you realize that this was the kick-in-the-pants you needed to start a new career. Many people in successful counseling careers have used the experience of helping others as a way to heal the wounds of a conflicted or unhappy childhood. Writers and artists routinely transform conflict into works of lasting beauty and value.

Take the example of Candy Lightner, whose daughter was killed by a drunk driver. She could have become overwhelmingly depressed and bitter as a result of her tragedy. Instead, she channelled her rage, founding Mothers Against Drunk Driving. This isn't to say that her pain was any less real — only that she chose not to let it immobilize her, and squeezed something good out of her tragedy.

Such people help you realize that events can't really make you feel or behave in any particular way. Candy Lightner's example teaches that your response to events is largely a matter of your own choosing.

Events alone don't cause feelings. Your thoughts and beliefs are the intervening mechanisms that determine how you feel.

Look at the diagram below. There is a dotted line between events (A) and feelings (C), suggesting an indirect connection. Your thoughts or beliefs (B) always intervene as a "detour" between events (A) and feelings (C).

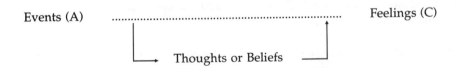

Feelings are the result not only of events but also of the combination of events, *plus* what you think or believe. Look at the following three examples. Each has been chosen to illustrate one of the key beliefs that contribute to bad feelings.

1. Raoul wants to borrow his father's convertible to take his new girlfriend for a drive in the country. His father says no. Raoul feels upset because of the refusal *plus* the fact that he believes the convertible to be essential to the success of his outing.

2. Sonia learns that her sister-in-law, whom Sonia has always admired, has been bad-mouthing her behind her back. Sonia feels this as a terrible blow to her self-esteem. Her feelings are the result of her sister-in-law's behavior *plus* Sonia's long-held belief that her self-worth depends on the love of those she admires.

3. Peter is interested in working for the post office. He buys a study guide for the post office exam and studies for several weeks, but winds up doing poorly. Peter feels frustrated and angry because he believes that he must succeed at everything he tries hard to do.

In most such examples, the person experiencing the negative emotion believes that things *must* go his or her way. Long-held beliefs that cause you to suffer often have the word *must* in them: *I must get my way, I must be liked, I must succeed.*

By holding on to *must* beliefs, we abuse ourselves. Albert Ellis, upon whose work cognitive therapy is based, calls such thinking "musterbation," a form of self-abuse! His pun is insightful, because he implies that by getting rid of "musts," you can stop abusing yourself. That is, you can stop setting yourself up to be unhappy, angry, anxious, or depressed.

Must statements about risk-taking usually engender anxiety. Although the wording may vary slightly from case to case, a *must* statement is always in some way tied to experience that triggers a negative emotion.

Below are the three general types of *must* statements. In the right-hand column is the type of anxiety triggered by each type of *must* statement. The examples are those of Raoul, Sonia, and Peter.

Example	*Must* Statement	Type of Anxiety
Raoul and his father's car	*I must get all my needs met.*	Frustration anxiety
Sonia and her sister-in-law	*I must be liked by everyone.*	Acceptance anxiety
Peter and the post office exam	*I must succeed at everything I try to accomplish.*	Performance anxiety

Getting Rid of the Musts

What happens when you replace *must* statements with preference statements? Everything changes.

For example, "I must succeed at everything I try to accomplish" becomes, "It would be nice if I succeeded at everything I tried to accomplish — but my personal worth and happiness doesn't depend on it." "I must get all my needs met" becomes, "It would be terrific if my needs were always met, but I can still be happy when things don't go just my way."

Preferences aren't necessities. When you formulate them, you don't allow your contentment to depend on events over which you have, at best, limited control.

When you experience a negative emotion, try to uncover the *must* statement that is contributing to it. Argue with yourself. For example, ask yourself, "Is it really a matter of life and death that everyone like me? Does my happiness depend on my succeeding at everything I set out to accomplish?" Once you expose your inner thoughts, try substituting a preference statement for every *must*. By doing that you take charge of your emotions.

Exercise: Recognizing and Replacing Must Statements

Below are three problematic situations. Each results in feelings of anxiety. Find the *must* statement at the heart of the person's reaction. Write it down in the space provided. Then write down the corresponding type or types of anxiety (frustration, acceptance, performance). Finally, formulate a preference statement. Sample answers follow the exercise.

> **Situation One:** Barbara, a college student, wants to become an actress. When she hears that there will be auditions for a student production of Arthur Miller's *The Crucible*, she gets hold of a copy of the play and studies it carefully. She tries out for the part of Abigail, but is offered a part in the chorus instead. When auditions are held for the student production the following season, Barbara would like to try out for the lead, but feels reluctant to risk the trauma of another rejection.
>
> *Must* Statement: _____
>
> Type(s) of Anxiety: _____
>
> Preference Statement: _____
>
> _____

Sample Answers for Situation One:

Must Statement: I must succeed at everything I try (in this case, getting the lead).

Type(s) of Anxiety: Performance, acceptance

Preference Statement: It would be nice if I succeeded in getting every part I tried out for, but my happiness doesn't depend on it — and my future as an actress doesn't depend on my getting the lead in any particular play.

Situation Two: Janice and Stefan moved into their suburban home two years ago. Since then, they've made it a point to be friendly to their immediate neighbors, the Dawsons. They've collected mail when the Dawsons were away. They had the Dawsons over for dinner while some work was being done on their kitchen. Stefan lent them his chainsaw for some yardwork. When the Dawsons throw a party and don't invite Janice and Stefan, they feel hurt and resentful.

Must Statement: _____

Type(s) of Anxiety: _____

Preference Statement: _____

_____

Sample Answers for Situation Two:

Must Statement: We must be liked by everyone (in this case, we must be invited to our neighbor's party).

Type(s) of Anxiety: Acceptance

Preference Statement: It would be nice if everybody liked us and if the Dawsons invited us to their party, but our happiness doesn't depend on it.

Situation Three: Benny, who never had the chance for an education, believes that his success as a father depends on his son attending college. He tries hard to convince his son, a senior in high school, that a college degree is a necessary credential. He takes his son to different campuses, attends open houses with him, even writes away for applications. In the end, Benny's son admits that he wants to go to trade school to learn to be an auto mechanic — just like his father. Benny feels depressed and thwarted.

Must Statement: _____

Type(s) of Anxiety: _____

Preference Statement: _____

_____

Sample answers for Situation Three

Must Statement: I must get all my needs met (in this case, the need to have my son go to college to fulfill my expectations of myself as a father).

Type(s) of Anxiety: Frustration

Preference Statement: It would be nice if this need were met — it's been my life's dream to have a son who graduated from college. But my son is an individual who has to make his own choices; and his choices don't determine my success as a father. (*Mine* do!)

Risk-Taking and Anxiety

How does all this apply to risk-taking? Most people — and you're probably one of them — avoid taking risks because they experience one or more of the types of anxiety identified in the examples above. People avoid risks because of the *must* statements echoing in their heads.

Below are three examples of the relationship between risks and the anxieties defined by the psychologist Albert Ellis. Suggestions follow on how to use Ellis' methods to overcome your reluctance to risk. In each case, the reluctance is traced back to its origins in a *must* statement. Overcoming your reluctance requires replacing the *must* statement with a preference statement.

Performance Anxiety. This involves any self-improvement risk that carries the possibility of failure. The accompanying *must* statement is, "I must succeed at everything I try."

If you believe that you must succeed at everything you try, you'll be afraid to put yourself to the test by taking risks. The possibility of failure will be just too threatening.

The resulting indecisiveness may paralyze your personal life and career. You may find yourself toying with ideas but never acting on them. If you make a decision, you second-guess yourself unmercifully about whether you made the *right* decision. In this state of emotional paralysis, you may believe that a wrong decision has irreversible, even fatal, consequences.

Instead of learning new skills or developing new talents, you may stick to what you already know, and miss many opportunities for pleasure and self-expansion. Your dread of failure may be debilitating. This may be particularly true if your sense of personal worth is tied up with achievement. Perhaps your parents were overbearing perfectionists. Whatever the reason, the effect is to narrow your world dramatically. (There is more specific information on this topic in Chapter 4.)

A person who believes that he or she must succeed at everything will probably avoid learning new skills. Take the example of learning to sail. A beginner sailor must accept the fact that he or she may find it hard to manage sheets and tiller, is likely to capsize, and perhaps will be laughed at by others.

The solution is to recognize the *must* statement that you carry around in your head. Substitute with a preference statement: "It would be nice if I could learn to sail without appearing foolish. But that's not realistic; nor does my self-esteem depend on it." Work on developing an open attitude toward learning. Remember, failure is best seen as an opportunity to learn.

Acceptance Anxiety. This involves any self-disclosure risks or commitment risks likely to trigger the disapproval of others. The accompanying *must* statement is, "I must be liked by everyone."

If you believe that you must be liked by everyone, your sense of personal worth is too bound up with others' approval: if your self-esteem depends on what others think of you, you haven't got any. People who lack a strong sense of self-worth are often unwilling to do anything that might displease others — including expressing their opinions freely, setting their own priorities, and so on.

By being too concerned about the opinions of others, you lose yourself and become nothing more than a reflection of what others expect of you. You'll become so good at blending into the woodwork that people will forget you're there. Resentment and rage are the inevitable consequences: even though these feelings may go unexpressed, and may never even be consciously felt, they will eventually take their toll. Ironically, your desire to win the regard and approval of others is more likely to have the opposite effect: your needs will be overlooked; you're bound to be ignored, taken for granted, and unappreciated.

If you're afraid to displease others, you're probably unwilling to express your opinions and let others know what you think unless you're certain that you won't risk their disapproval.

If you avoid doing things for fear of displeasing others, rid yourself of the *must* statement that dominates your thinking. Substitute a preference statement, such as: "It would be nice if everyone liked me no matter what I said or did, but that's not realistic. Anyway, I can survive and even prosper without pleasing everyone." Take the time you need to accept this statement as true. Then gradually begin taking the risks associated with revealing yourself.

Frustration Anxiety. This involves any commitment risks or self-improvement risks requiring personal sacrifice. The accompanying *must* statement is, "I must get all my needs met."

If you believe that you must get all your needs met, you'll be unwilling to make the personal and financial sacrifices necessary to realize your dreams and ambitions.

For example, you may be unwilling to quit a secure but dull job to take a more exciting one that's less secure; or you might hesitate to open a business that might be less secure than your present work situation but more stimulating and personally satisfying.

The way out of this bind is to recognize the role of frustration anxiety in your unwillingness to make the sacrifices necessary to realize your dreams. After you've uncovered your individual *must* statement, substitute a preference statement such as, "It would be nice if I could realize my dreams while continuing to have all my needs met." Think hard about it. Isn't it true that you could survive without all the comforts (and security) you're used to?

Give yourself several weeks to refashion your thinking, until you feel convinced that you can make the sacrifices necessary to achieve what you want. Then slowly experiment with depriving yourself of things or feelings you're used to having. Gradually build your tolerance to frustration, until your anticipated reaction to discomfort and deprivation no longer interferes with your efforts to realize your dreams.

Identifying and Replacing Your Own Must Statements

Now that you have a good grasp of the relationship between risk-taking and the three key anxieties, it's time to put this knowledge to work in your own life.

In the worksheet that follows, identify the *musts* that keep you from taking risks; then refute them and replace them with preference statements. Make several photocopies of this worksheet before you begin (or copy the headings onto a blank sheet of paper).

How To Use the Worksheet. First, describe three risks you would like to take. (Refer to your Personal Risk Profile in Chapter 3.) In the second column, identify the *must* statement that keeps you from taking each risk. (If there is more than one *must* statement, rank them in order of their importance. Then fill out the chart for each *must* statement.) In the third column, note the kind of anxiety or other feelings engendered by each *must* statement. If there's more than one "must," identify the feeling triggered by each one. In the fourth column, replace the *must* statement with a preference statement that includes

Worksheet:
Banishing the *Musts* That Keep Me From Taking Desired Risks

Risk I'm Avoiding:

1. _____

2. _____

3. _____

Risk	Accompanying *Must* Statement(s)	Type of Anxiety or Other Feelings Engendered	Refutation and Preference Statement I Can Use Instead
1.			
2.			
3.			

On the next page is an example of a completed worksheet.

Worksheet:
Banishing the *Musts* That Keep Me From Taking Desired Risks

Risks I'm Avoiding:

1. Looking for a better job

2. Asking Robin whether we should move in together

3. Getting involved in the pro-choice movement

Risk	Accompanying *Must* Statement(s)	Type of Anxiety or Other Feelings Engendered	Refutation and Preference Statement I Can Use Instead
1.	I must succeed at everything I try to do.	Performance anxiety: If I don't manage to find a better job, everyone will know I'm a loser.	It's okay to try and fail sometimes. If I don't try new things, I'll never get anywhere. Other people will respect my courage for taking risks — but, more importantly, I'll respect myself.
2.	I must be loved and accepted by everyone.	Acceptance anxiety: My self-esteem depends on Robin welcoming this next step in our relationship.	I'm a good and lovable person whether or not Robin wants us to move in together just now. Robin's feelings don't determine my basic worth as a human being. It would be nice if Robin's wants and needs were in sync with mine all the time; but it's unrealistic to expect this to be the case.
3.	I must get all my work done and continue to meet my high standards in everything I do.	Frustration anxiety: If I add one more thing to my agenda, I'm going to fall down somewhere — the house will be a pig sty, the kids will go to the dogs, my husband will feel ignored, my boss will look for a replacement for me.	I'm allowed to do a less-than-perfect job sometimes. It would be great if I could be superwoman, but I'm only human. If getting involved in something I believe in means relaxing my standards somewhat, then it's up to me to decide whether or not the tradeoff is acceptable.

a refutation. When writing these, pretend you're a courtroom lawyer presenting your closing argument to the jury: make your refutation convincing.

By identifying your thoughts that induce feelings of self-defeat, you can free yourself from their clutches. You will be more able to behave rationally and control the way you feel by imposing discipline on the way you think.

Developments in Cognitive Therapy

The ideas and self-help techniques you just learned were developed by Albert Ellis many years ago. Since then, the techniques have been refined and built upon by scores of other practitioners. So-called cognitive therapists — therapists who are concerned with the way your thinking affects your feelings and behavior — have identified several common kinds of distorted thinking, along with ways in which you can conveniently and systematically refute the thoughts that distress, frustrate, frighten, or inhibit you.

Cognitive Distortions

In Chapter 4, you learned about the common logical distortions, and that specific distortions, as well as immobilizing thoughts, are associated with specific fears. As you read the annotated list of distortions below, keep in mind their relationship to your own inhibitions about risk-taking.

All-or-Nothing Thinking (also known as Polarized Thinking). This involves seeing things in absolute terms, as either black or white, with no shades of gray in between. Any risk that doesn't result in a total success is seen as a total failure.

Blaming. If you indulge in this particular distortion, you waste time, energy, and your chance for insight by blaming yourself or others when things go wrong. Instead of figuring out what went wrong from your failure, and trying again, you find distraction from your painful feelings by placing blame. Blaming others is a way to pretend that you have no control over your situation — as well as an excuse for avoiding similar risks in the future.

Catastrophizing (also known as Awfulizing). When you catastrophize, you unrealistically inflate the importance or severity of an event or its outcomes. For example, you predict that the most serious and horrible consequences will follow from your actions. In doing this, you magnify the importance of your particular set of circumstances until they assume life-and-death proportions. If you have to confront your boss about something, you blow the event and its possible consequences way out of proportion. "I can't risk antagonizing my boss; if I do, I'll lose my job and wind up living on the streets." This kind of thinking tends to have a snowball effect, with each new thought feeding your catastrophic vision of ruin and despair.

Minimizing. When you minimize, you fail to take sufficient pride in personal accomplishments and successes; instead, you dismiss them as unimportant. You may have succeeded in risk-taking many times; but when a risk fails, you're likely to lend that failure a disproportionate weight. You minimize your past accomplishments, making them seem trivial in the overall pattern of your successes and failures: "Yes, I did such-and-such, but anyone could have done that."

The antidote to both catastrophizing and minimizing is balance. Place failures and disappointments in perspective, without dismissing your successes and accomplishments. It's also important to gauge risks rationally, weighing the likely consequences of your actions. How likely is it that confronting your boss will result in the loss of your job? And if you do lose your job, how likely is it that you'll never work again? What circumstances would have to conspire before you would really be living on the street?

Fortune-telling. If you practice this cognitive distortion, you predict the worst possible outcome; in modern parlance, this is called "programming a disaster." Your mind concocts a worst-case scenario; and you waltz into your future *expecting* this outcome. As if you had been programmed like a computer, your expectations will often determine the outcome of any given situation involving your behavior. For example, a woman might be convinced that if she were to risk admitting that she's sexually attracted to a male friend, he'd think less of her: "If I tell him I'm sexually attracted to him, he'll think I'm a slut." Because of her expectation, she may actually color her disclosure in such a way that the man *does* end up thinking less of her. This is also spoken of as a "self-fulfilling prophecy."

It's far more productive to anticipate positive outcomes when your own skill or behavior is involved. At the very least, consider all possible outcomes, weigh their probability, and make contingency plans.

Labeling. If you're a labeler, chances are that you don't look at your weaknesses and errors as opportunities for self-improvement; instead, you get down on yourself and call yourself names. "Everyone else has more friends than I do," you're likely to say to yourself after you've risked inviting someone out and been turned down. "No one cares about me. I'm a loser." Labels have an awful way of "freezing" reality. They take on a life of their own, often making change extremely difficult. Instead of judging and labeling, try using precise descriptive terms that apply to a given situation: "Ellen said that she was busy on Thursday night"; "Mark looked at his watch twice while I was giving my presentation." This is far more benign than telling yourself "I'm a reject and a bore!"

Mental Filtering (also known as Tunnel Vision). If your thinking is distorted by a mental filter, you disregard positive perceptions and focus only on what's negative. You may have a history of successful risk-taking, but one disappointment will cause you to filter out all the successes. This is similar to minimizing. You allow your one disappointment to unfairly color your perceptions of the past. With many people, this distortion makes them virtually unable to hear a compliment, whereas every little criticism comes in loud and clear.

Mind Reading. This is actually quite an arrogant distortion. You interpret other people's behavior based on your assumptions about what they're thinking. If Ellen turns you down for Thursday night, you assume that it's because she thinks you're a nerd (not because she sees her therapist on Thursday evenings); if Mark looks at his watch, it's because he thinks you're boring (not because his sister on the West Coast has just had surgery and he's trying to figure out how soon he can phone her). As a self-conscious adult beginner on the ski slopes at a crowded ski resort, you might say to yourself, "Everyone's probably laughing at me." But how do you know that to be true? Some observers, more timid than you, might just as likely be admiring your courage. Others, perhaps experienced skiers, might just as well be feeling empathy for you. More likely, the other skiers are involved in their own experiences, and aren't thinking about you at all.

Overgeneralization. If you are tripped up by this fallacy, you see one failure or disappointment as proof that you're doomed to a life of unhappiness. For example, if you lost your job, you might say, "Getting fired from my job means that I'm a deficient human being; I'll never work again." If your spouse suggests that you not wear a particular shirt to a party, you might overgeneralize from that one statement that your spouse hates the way you dress. As with the cognitive distortion of labeling, overgeneralization is best defeated by precision in the way you tell yourself the story of what's happening in your life.

Should Statements. Every *should* statement, whether it's imposed on you by yourself or somebody else, carries a judgment and an expectation. When others tell you what you should do, it sounds as though they really know — that they're merely serving as spokesperson for some eternal law that has come down from heaven: "You should call your mother weekly!" "You should join a fraternity!" "You should act your age!" The truth is, except in technical and legal matters (when there really are objective requirements that must be met), these people are doing nothing more than expressing their own preferences and opinions and imposing them on you.

Perhaps you impose *should* statements on yourself: "I should be a good daughter/son," or "I should always be polite and kind." Many people look backward and torture themselves with regrets: "I should have said that!" "I could have done this." "If I'd only known, I would have acted differently!"

Should statements can inhibit all three types of risk-taking. A middle-aged man with a yen for motorcycling might never take the self-fulfillment risk of enjoying the sport because he wouldn't want to appear foolish, or crude, or adolescent. After all, we should all act our age, right? A woman might not take the self-disclosure risk of telling off her boss because she's been brought up to believe that she should always be polite and kind. Another person might avoid the commitment risk of participating in an antiwar rally because he believes that he should always act in the manner of a law-abiding citizen.

Selective Interpretation.   When this cognitive distortion warps your thinking, you take an event or a comment out of context to arrive at an interpretation that's not supported by the larger body of facts. (This is similar to quoting someone out of context.) You might see an individual's momentary look of displeasure and read into it global, immutable disapproval of you and all you stand for. No doubt, during an unpleasant confrontation, the person you're talking with will be displeased. But in the vast majority of cases, the displeasure passes with time. If you fail to see that, you will be haunted by the fear and dread that once you evoke another's displeasure, there is nothing you can do to redeem yourself. The effect of this kind of thinking is to discourage you from taking any risks that might evoke the displeasure of others.

Personalization.   This arises from the tendency to see all of life as a struggle in which others or even circumstances are continually trying to upset, frustrate, discourage, or humiliate you. One junior faculty member serving on her first important academic committee spent hours in the library researching the subject of the committee's deliberations. She found a wonderful article in a scholarly journal, replete with facts that committee members would find extremely helpful. She duplicated the article at her own expense, painstakingly composed a cover letter addressed to the chairperson of the committee, and sent the entire package to him for distribution to members. At the next meeting, she expected that the materials would be discussed at length and anticipated that her hard work would be warmly acknowledged. Instead, no one acknowledged her contribution. Crushed, she saw the committee's lack of reaction as proof of their determination to frustrate her academic career. The fact was, the chairperson had accepted a job at another university and was just going through the motions of his present job; he was not very involved at all in the committee's work. He distributed the materials without giving a moment's thought to the work they represented. The other members had no idea where the materials came from.

Obviously, taking things personally can lead to erroneous conclusions. It can also discourage risk-taking by fostering negative expectations and creating unnecessary psychological pressure.

Reasoning With Your Heart (also known as Emotional Reasoning and Subjective Reasoning). This distortion occurs when you assume that your negative emotions are a reliable indicator of the way things really are. For example, because you feel like a failure, you must be one. Because you feel anxious and discouraged about taking a particular risk, you're convinced that your goal is impossible to accomplish.

Over-Responsibility. When you're burdened by this distorted way of thinking, you grossly exaggerate your role in bringing about some undesirable outcome. For example, if a youngster gets into trouble at school or runs afoul of the law, a parent might take responsibility: "If I were a better father, my son would never have done this. It's all my fault!" Risk-takers most often fall victim to this distortion when they anticipate outcomes, and blame themselves for whatever happens: "If I move out on my own, my parents will be devastated, and it'll be all my fault!"

Overcoming Distorted Thinking

Follow the procedures below (using the worksheets as a guide) to acquire skill in identifying your immobilizing thoughts and the cognitive distortions that lie beneath them. Make several copies of the blank worksheet, or copy the headings onto sheets of lined paper.

Here's how to use the worksheet. Begin by describing the high-risk desires, wishes, or ambitions you want to pursue. List these by numbers.

For each risk, ferret out the immobilizing, fear-inducing thoughts that go through your head when you contemplate the risk. Write these down in the second column.

Next, identify the distortions at the heart of your immobilizing thoughts. Write these down in the third column. If you're having trouble with this step, review the descriptions of the 14 cognitive distortions in the preceding pages. A series of questions to help you identify each distortion follows below.

The final step is to formulate rational, positive, and realistic refutations of your distorted thinking. Consider these comebacks carefully, then write them down in the right-hand column.

Using this worksheet can help you overcome your fear of risk-taking one risk at a time. Do the exercise whenever your fears are inhibiting you from taking a chance or going for the brass ring.

Simply saying these things to yourself will not have the same effect as putting them down on paper. Do the exercise in writing every time. By repeating this process often, you can free yourself to fulfill your every ambition — or at least give your every ambition your best shot.

Questions To Help You Identify Cognitive Distortions:

1. Have I reduced some complex reality to black-and-white or all-or-nothing alternatives? *(All-or-nothing thinking)*

2. Have I responded to a setback by blaming either myself, someone else, or circumstances instead of seeing it as an opportunity to learn? *(Blaming)*

3. Have I distorted some unwanted outcome as a catastrophe I simply couldn't survive? *(Catastrophizing)*

4. Have I downplayed or trivialized my accomplishments or successes? *(Minimizing)*

5. Have I predicted some unwanted outcome without having any solid basis on which to make the prediction? *(Fortune-telling)*

6. Have I called anyone a name or described myself or someone else in unflattering terms? *(Labeling)*

7. Have I blocked out my past successes or my talents and focused instead on some negative experience or quality? *(Mental filter)*

8. Have I presumed to know how others must be thinking or feeling? *(Mind reading)*

9. Have I taken one or a small number of unwanted experiences as proof that I'm condemned forever to repeat them? *(Overgeneralization)*

10. Have I allowed my arbitrary expectations of myself (or those of others) to cloud my thinking about how I feel or what I want? *(Should statements)*

11. Have I taken some event or reaction out of context and jumped to a conclusion that's not supported by the larger body of facts? *(Selective interpretation)*

12. Have I come to believe that others are deliberately setting out to humiliate, disappoint, or frustrate me? *(Personalization)*

13. Have I used my feelings exclusively to draw a conclusion about the truth? *(Reasoning with your heart)*

14. Have I taken responsibility for something over which I have little or no control? *(Over-responsibility)*

All the methods described in this chapter can be used singly or together. They can also be combined with the behavioral methods discussed in Chapter 5, the threshold method and systematic desensitization.

Worksheet:
Overcoming Distorted Thinking

The risks I plan to take:

1. _____

2. _____

3. _____

Risk	Immobilizing, Fear-Inducing Thoughts	Relevant Cognitive Distortions	Refutations or Rational Comebacks
1.			
2.			
3.			

Sample Worksheet:
Overcoming Distorted Thinking

The risks I plan to take:

1. Ask Katrina out for a date.

2. Quit nursing and open a business that will allow me to make a lot of money.

3. _____

Risk	Immobilizing, Fear-Inducing Thoughts	Relevant Cognitive Distortions	Refutations or Rational Comebacks
1.	She'll probably laugh at me and make me feel like a jerk.	Fortune-telling	I don't know for certain that she'll laugh at me. She might even accept. Even if she doesn't, though, I'll survive. If she turns me down, I can conduct myself in a way that won't make me feel like a jerk. I'll be gracious, no matter what.
	I'm a pretty dull guy. Why would an attractive woman like Katrina want to go out with a loser like me?	Labeling: I'm characterizing myself as "dull" and "a loser."	I'm about as interesting as a lot of guys I know, and I'm more interesting than some of them. There's no such thing as a 100% certified loser. Different people have different ideas about what's attractive. Who knows — maybe Katrina will be delighted to go out with me. Maybe she's so pretty that no one asks her out — they're all intimidated!
2.	I shouldn't place so much emphasis on making money. Whatever happened to my values? At one time I used to think it was important to help people.	Should statement: I'm putting myself down for wanting to make a lot of money, as though by doing that I'd be violating some rule that's set in stone: "Good people shouldn't make a lot of money."	First of all, what's wrong in making money? I'm not getting any younger, and I need to provide for myself adequately. I don't want to wind up poor when I'm old. Secondly, it's wrong to see making money as the polar opposite to helping people. It's possible to make money while helping others. People in business don't survive very long if they don't help thier customers!

Sample Worksheet:
Overcoming Distorted Thinking

page 2

Risk	Immobilizing, Fear-Inducing, Thoughts	Relevant Cognitive Distortions	Refutations or Rational Comebacks
2. (cont.)	My family and friends will think less of me for giving up on caring for people and trying to make a lot of money.	Mind reading; All-or-nothing thinking	I can't really know what other people are thinking! And I'm not responsible for what they think, anyway. I can only be responsible for my own thoughts and feelings. As noted above, caring for people and making money are not necessarily mutually exclusive propositions: I can be a caring person and still make a good living.
	If I quit, some of the younger nurses who look up to me will become dis-illusioned with nursing and may decide to leave, too.	Over-responsibility	It's unfair to hold myself responsible for anyone's career decision but my own.

Further Reading

Ellis, A. (1977) *How To Live With and Without Anger.* New York: Reader's Digest Press.
Ellis, A., and Harper, R.A. (1975) *A New Guide to Rational Living.* North Hollywood, CA: Wilshire Book Co.

7

How To Prepare for
Taking Risks

What You Hope for When You Risk

To risk successfully, you need insight into your own fears, and knowledge about how to overcome them. This chapter gives a systematic approach to risk-taking that will allow you to become thoroughly prepared before putting yourself on the line.

Your preparation depends on the outcome you want to achieve. There are only two categories of outcomes, and one of them always predominates in every risky venture.

Overt Personal Benefit

Does your risk involve an overt, practical, personal benefit? The examples below fall into this first category of possible outcomes.

- You might want to improve your relationship with someone. In Chapter 3, we used the example of Peter, who sought a more satisfying sex life with his partner. He had to take the self-disclosure risk of expressing his dissatisfaction in order to bring about the improvement he wanted.

- You might want to better your life in some material way. Perhaps you'll enter a competition in the hope of gaining personal recognition or winning a scholarship to a program you might not otherwise be able to afford. These ends can only be accomplished by taking the self-improvement risk of competing.

- You may want to change your career or pursue opportunities that are closed to you now. For example, you may decide to return to school or apply for a new job. Once again, you must take a self-improvement risk to achieve your goal.

Other Outcomes

The other category of outcomes is a grab bag for all goals that do not involve an overt, practical, personal benefit. These include risks of a more selfless or idealistic nature. For instance:

- You might choose to become involved in a particular cause to help right a wrong or join those who are speaking out on behalf of an important principle. Perhaps you'll participate in a demonstration, volunteer to serve as a witness at a trial or work at a center for the homeless, or become an auxiliary police officer to fight crime in your city or town. In all such cases, you are taking a commitment risk, standing up for something you believe in.

- You might seek to improve yourself in some way, but not because you'll gain any material or even any tangible benefit. For example, you might take art or music lessons, join a book club, or take adult courses at a local college to deepen your knowledge of the world. Of course, there are many hidden benefits associated with such self-improvement risks; and even though they may not make you more money or yield any other tangible benefit, they have a great deal of potential to change your life for the better.

There are two basic sets of procedures that will prepare you as thoroughly as possible for the two categories of risks discussed above. Procedure One is appropriate when you're planning to take a risk because you hope to benefit personally in some tangible way. When you're risking for some other reason, follow Procedure Two. It's to your advantage to become familiar with both procedures.

Procedure One: Risks With Practical Benefits

When your objective in risking is practical, you need to analyze the problem you're facing. There are four steps involved in that analysis:

1. Define the problem

2. Set goals

3. Analyse the risk

4. Conduct a "what-if" analysis

Define the Problem

The dictionary defines a problem as "a question proposed for solution; hence a perplexing question, situation, or person." Not every problem requires risk-taking. Some, like algebra problems, require straightforward calculations. But most human problems demand more than that. To deal effectively with them, you may have to take chances.

When you take a risk, you'll increase your chances of a successful outcome by learning as much as possible about the problem involved, what you want to have happen, and what you might lose.

Almost every problem begins with a feeling of dissatisfaction. Sometimes the reason is very apparent. At other times the reason isn't entirely clear. You may feel displeased with your job, without knowing why. You may feel restless and bored with your spouse or partner, but not know the exact reason. In such cases, you need to follow specific steps to uncover the reason for your dissatisfaction, plan a response, and formulate a course of action.

When you sense that something is wrong, begin identifying the sources of your dissatisfaction. Ask yourself these questions:

- What should be happening now that isn't?

- What is actually happening now that shouldn't be happening?

- In the best of all possible worlds, what could be happening?

Let's assume, for example, that you're dissatisfied in an important relationship. Follow the formula above and answer these questions:

- What should be happening in the relationship that isn't? What am I looking for from my partner? Why am I not getting?

- What is happening in the relationship that I don't like? What changes have to occur in the relationship for me to be happier?

- Under ideal circumstances, what would be happening in this relationship?

There is absolutely nothing wrong with trying to influence a partner to satisfy your needs more completely in a relationship. You initially formed the relationship because you saw it as a way of satisfying some of your needs. When it no longer satisfies enough of your needs, you have a responsibility to yourself and your partner to let that be known, and to influence his or her behavior so that the relationship meets more of your needs.

Of course, you should reformulate these questions to make them relevant to the dissatisfaction you're feeling (for instance, "What should be happening in my job that isn't?").

Sketching the history of the problem is often useful. Ask yourself these questions:

- How did the problem come about?
- What past events have shaped it?
- Have I made any attempts to solve the problem?
- Have they brought about any improvement?
- Why haven't they succeeded completely?

In some cases, recalling how a problem came about can help you understand it. For example, it's often very difficult to resolve an interpersonal problem without reviewing the misunderstandings and hurt feelings that caused it to occur.

Ask yourself, *What would happen if I did nothing?* To get a handle on the problem that beckons you to risk, ask yourself what would happen if you did absolutely nothing. Do you think the situation would get better, worse, or stay the same? Three months down the road, what would you be experiencing?

Sometimes it's wise to wait out a situation, because some problems resolve themselves. But be careful. Waiting can amount to "deciding not to decide." It can also be a way of deciding against something without really accepting responsibility for the decision. Suppose, for example, that while working at one job, you are offered another. Your failure to respond will usually be taken as a decision to stay put. In this case, not acting is equivalent to deciding to decline the offer.

Exercise 1: Defining Your Problem

To build your skills in defining problems that require risk-taking, choose a current problem in your life. The problem should be a source of moderate distress to you, and its solution should require some action on your part. You will be working with this problem throughout the rest of this chapter — so choose something meaningful.

Begin examining the problem by following these guidelines (use extra paper if you need it):

Identify the source of your distress.
If you know why you're dissatisfied, write the reason here:

If you aren't sure why you're dissatisfied, answer each of the following questions:
- What should be happening now that isn't?

- What is actually happening now that shouldn't be happening?

- In the best of all possible worlds, what could be happening?

To deepen your understanding of the problem, trace its origins.
- How did the problem come about? Over how long a period of time?

- Who has been (and is) part of the problem? If other people are involved, how does each person contribute to making it worse?

- What are my motivations for continuing in this situation?

- What might be the motivations of other people involved in this problem?

Finally, ask yourself what would happen if you did absolutely nothing.

- Will the problem resolve itself if I do nothing?

- What human, financial, or other costs will I pay if I just let things alone?

Set Goals

Before taking any risk, it's essential to formulate clear goals. Ask yourself what you hope to accomplish by your action. It's best to state your goal in the form of a *to* statement: "to increase my earnings by at least $10,000 per year," "to see whether Jim is interested in dating me," "to get my brother to help out more in caring for our elderly parents."

Make your *to* statement brief and to the point, but clear enough to spell out what you want to accomplish. You need a clear goal in order to evaluate your progress and judge the success of your risk-taking.

Exercise 2: Setting Your Goal

Working with the problem you identified in Exercise 1, formulate a goal that spells out what you want to achieve (write your goal in the form of a *to* statement). Remember, when you achieve your goal, your problem will be over: you will have gotten precisely what you want. Write your goal statement here:

Analyse the Risk

To analyse your risk, spell out potential gains and losses. The key questions you must ask yourself are

- What do I stand to gain when I risk?

- What might I lose?

Investors do this when they estimate downside risk and upside potential. An investor who buys real estate in a depressed but up-and-coming area has little downside risk but a great deal of upside potential. On the other hand, an investor who buys property at an all-time high assumes a lot of downside risk, but can expect relatively little upside potential.

The same principles apply in your personal risk-taking: your emotional risks have both an up side and a down side. If you stand to lose very little but gain a lot, then your downside risk is minimal, but your upside potential is great. This may be the case when you decide to risk insisting on changes in an unsatisfying relationship.

There's usually little personal benefit derived from maintaining your commitment to an unsatisfying relationship. It is true, however, that there may be perceived benefits. An unhappily married couple may decide to stay together "for the sake of the children." The same phenomenon operates when a person remains in an unsatisfying job because "the pay is good."

Perceived benefits aside, when a relationship isn't working, there's relatively little downside risk associated with confronting your partner and insisting on changes. (If you stand to gain little from your risk-taking but to lose a lot, you are taking a selfless risk. There will be more about this under Procedure Two.)

Your boldness as a risk-taker is determined by your willingness to tolerate significant downside risk in face of significant upside potential. When Walt Disney proposed the first full-length cartoon, every advisor he consulted cautioned him against it: "Too risky," they said, "audiences won't go for it." But Disney was willing to risk ridicule and dollars because he believed in an idea. History proved him right. The upside potential was fully realized, and his career was made.

Here are some guidelines to use in calculating your upside and downside potential:

- What do I stand to gain by taking this risk?

- What is the likelihood of that gain being realized?

- Do past experience and common sense indicate that the odds are in my favor?

- Are the odds at least acceptable?

- What would I lose if I took this risk and it failed totally?
- How much am I willing to put "on the line"?
- What is the likelihood of total failure? Of partial success?
- Would I be willing to settle for a partial success?

Exercise 3: Analysing Your Risk

Examine the problem you've been working with, and consider the action you intend to take to solve it. Then weigh the potential costs and benefits of your action. To do so systematically, answer these questions:

What risky action am I planning to take?

What do I stand to gain by taking this risk?

- What is the likelihood of that gain being realized?

- Do past experiences and common sense indicate that the odds are in my favor? Are they at least acceptable?

What would I lose if I took this risk and it failed totally?

- How much am I willing to put "on the line"?

- What is the likelihood of total failure? Of partial success?

- Would I be willing to settle for partial success?

Note: If you are considering more than one course of action, take a separate piece of paper and follow these steps for each alternative under consideration.

Conduct a "What-if" Analysis

The fourth step in problem analysis involves identifying possible glitches that can develop in your risk-taking. By exploring possible outcomes, estimating their likelihood, and planning for them to the extent possible, you will give yourself a tremendous advantage in your risk-taking.

Exercise 4: Conducting a "What-if" Analysis

Construct a "what-if" analysis of the risky action you're considering. Write each potential problem in column 1. Estimate the probability of its occuring in column 2. Describe a plan of action in column 3. Make copies of the blank worksheet before you start, or copy the headings onto another sheet of paper. Following the blank worksheet, there's an example of one that's been filled out. You can use this as a guide.

"What-if" Analysis

Goal:

Potential Problem	Estimated Probability	Contingency Plan

Look at the example below to see how a "what-if" analysis can help you cover all the bases in your risk-taking. In the example, a woman, married with children, is considering returning to college.

Sample "What-if" Analysis

Goal: *To return to school and earn a bachelor's degree.*

Potential Problem	Estimated Probability	Contingency Plan
What will happen if I can't find the time to do the required work?	80%	I must talk with my family in advance to impress on them that my decision will require their cooperation in giving me the time I need.
Suppose I need to use the library but feel overwhelmed by the new, computerized research tools?	90%	As early in the semester as possible, I'll ask about a library orientation program for new and returning students.
I'll feel embarrassed at being the oldest person in the class.	60%	I'll introduce myself to each of the teachers and to a few students in every class. I'll let them know that I'm a returning student.

The same process can be followed in anticipating other problems: What if the kids get sick? What if I have to travel? And so on.

Conducting a "what-if" analysis reduces the element of chance in your risk-taking. And the less you leave to chance, the greater the likelihood of your success. It might surprise you to know that Philip Petit, the tightrope artist who walked across the gap between the Twin Towers of the World Trade Center in New York City, doesn't think of himself as a risk-taker. Why? Because he plans his high-wire stunts carefully and prepares for every eventuality. He comes as close as possible to eliminating accidents caused by chance! (See Ralph Keyes' *Chancing It*.)

Example of Four-Step Problem Analysis

Fran and Henry had been married for 23 years. For almost all of those years, Henry had been a teacher in an urban school district. Fran had worked for a corporation on the northern fringes of the city. She had risen through the ranks and earned a very good living as a purchasing manager. They had no children.

For a long time, the two had desired to move out of the city. They owned a small country home in a lake community about two-and-a-half hours away. They often fantasized about what it would be like to live there year round. But practical considerations — Henry's job and their comfortable lifestyle — had seduced them into staying in the city.

Then everything changed: Henry's school district offered long-term employees early retirement under very favorable terms. It was an offer that was too good to refuse. Suddenly, what had only been a dream became a real possibility.

Fran and Henry decided to act quickly. In the months before Henry's retirement, they hired contractors to redo their country cottage and convert it into a year-round home. Henry began looking into part-time work in their rural community. They replaced their older car with a brand-new one, as Fran would be spending more time than before on the road.

When moving day arrived, the two were buoyant. The more they thought about living in their lake community, the happier and more excited they became.

The first few months went by quickly. So many things needed to be done in the house. Fran took some vacation time so they could settle in. They enjoyed discovering new sights and taking early morning walks. They became involved socially and politically in their adopted community. Henry decided to run for the Board of Education. Fran volunteered to help out in their church Sunday school.

After Fran returned to work, the daily grind of her commute was mitigated somewhat by her pleasure in living in their new home. Nevertheless, she was bone-tired on many evenings; and, before long, she'd become so run down that she had to spend a week in bed. After her recovery, Fran was advised by a physician to rest as much as possible on weekends. After a few heart-to-heart talks, Fran and Henry agreed very reluctantly that the commute was simply too much for her. The dilemma they faced was serious. They loved their new lifestyle, but it was made possible to a large degree by Fran's salary. The two factors seemed mutually exclusive: Fran's salary and their wonderful new life in the country. On top of this, Fran had a twenty-year career with the corporation and a generous retirement policy down the road. She was not about to walk away from that without thinking very carefully.

They thought about renting an apartment near Fran's office, thinking that she could spend a few nights there to ease the burden of the commute. But neither of them wanted to spend so much time apart. They also considered moving closer to Fran's office; but after making all the renovations in their country home, they just couldn't bear to give it up.

Fran and Henry defined their problem: The burden of Fran's long commute created a dilemma. Either they had to sacrifice her income to enjoy their rual lifestyle, or sacrifice their lifestyle to enjoy Fran's earnings.

In response to their problem, they set their goal: to find a way to provide for themselves financially while enjoying their new life together in the country. They heard that the owners of the hardware store in town were retiring and putting the store up for sale. Fran and Henry began thinking. Perhaps they could buy the store and run it together.

The next step was to analyse the risk involved. They basically knew how much money they needed to live on. They spoke with the store owners and determined the net income they might expect from the store. They spoke with members of the chamber of commerce and with realtors; members of both groups foresaw a slow but steady population growth in the community. Perhaps, within a few years, the store could provide more than a simple living. There were no guarantees, of course. But more development was clearly in the planning stages.

Fran's experience as a purchasing manager would certainly be applicable to the needs of managing in the hardware store. So would Henry's nurturing personality and skill with people. He would enjoy the challenge of managing their own business; it would also give him a chance to supplement his retirement income. Both of them would enjoy the challenge.

Finally, they conducted a "what-if" analysis. They thought about the upside and the downside potential in owning the store. It seemed unlikely they could fail altogether. While they might not make a killing, their store was the only one in town, and for years it had generated a modest income for the previous owners. Furthermore, given the predictions of increased development, there would likely be a significant increase in demand for hardware products. They even considered putting new products on the shelves — things they had had to travel and buy as they set about putting the finishing touches on their converted cottage.

It was true that neither had ever run any kind of retail business before; but they were confident that they possessed many of the skills needed by businesspeople. They could also take advantage of resources offered by the Small Business Administration: counseling for small business owners and seminars held in conjunction with a nearby college.

They looked into financing the purchase. If they dipped into their savings and sold some of their common stock, they could make a substantial downpayment. Carrying the loan would not be too burdensome. Although it was possible that they could lose their investment, such a dire outcome seemed unlikely.

One last consideration occupied their minds. Despite the fact that the odds were in their favor, Fran was still reluctant to give up her job. She talked with her boss and negotiated a deal which left her the option of returning to the corporation if the new business did not pan out. By rolling over her accumulated retirement fund, she could protect much of it.

The last piece was in place.

Procedure Two: Risks Involving No Tangible Benefits

When your objective in risking is idealistic, your preparation isn't geared to ensuring success in the usual sense of the word. Where idealistic risks are concerned, you "succeed" by virtue of taking the chance, regardless of the outcome. It's still important to prepare for such risks systematically, even though the steps just described aren't exactly the ones you'll need to follow.

There's a second procedure for commitment and self-disclosure risks not intended to benefit you in some tangible way. This involves

1. Identifying the problem, opportunity, or distressing situation;

2. Examining your motivation;

3. Weighing the potential negative consequences of your action, and reducing them to a minimum.

Illustrative Example

Imagine for a moment that you're next in line at a checkout counter at a supermarket. The young man working the register is speaking to the woman in front of you as he bags her groceries. In the course of their conversation, he tells a joke that makes a particular ethnic group the butt of ridicule. They both laugh. The woman pays the bill, picks up her groceries, and leaves.

You are not amused. This was not a major Civil Rights violation, to be sure; not a crime. But what you heard was offensive. In fact, in your eyes, such thoughtlessness is an expression of ethnic prejudice.

You weigh the matter for a moment, realize that you might be thought odd if you say something, but decide to do it anyway. You have two options. One is to call the manager, angrily denounce the clerk, and ask that he be reprimanded. The other is to use the moment to try to raise this young man's consciousness by increasing his sensitivity to prejudice and its effects. You politely tell him that you found his joke offensive, and ask how he might feel if others told a joke that ridiculed him or his ethnic group. Without patronizing him or making a scene, you firmly express your view that such jokes promote prejudice and hurt innocent people.

An examination of your behavior shows that you followed each of the three steps mentioned earlier.

Define the Problem, Opportunity, or Distressing Situation

In the example, your witnessing the joke posed a problem for you. Should you speak out? If you did, you might be seen as a person who simply lacks a sense of humor. On the other hand, if you remained silent, your silence could be interpreted as condoning such tasteless humor. Just by virtue of your presence in a checkout line, you were confronted with a dilemma that demanded a response.

You've probably been confronted by such dilemmas many times in your life. The scale may have been small, as in the example. But it also may have been larger. For example, you may have witnessed co-workers stealing from your employer. You may know that members of your town's police department deliberately and consistently harass minority groups. You may realize that your best friend has a drinking problem. And so on. At the extreme end of seriousness, you may be a citizen of a country occupied by an invading force and be faced with the dilemma of whether to join the resistance. (This was the problem faced by French and Dutch citizens as well as those of other Nazi-occupied countries during World War II, and by the citizens of Kuwait during the Persian Gulf conflict.)

In all such cases, effective risking demands that you examine the situation. What principle is at stake? What harm would be done by your doing nothing? (In the '60s, a favorite saying among Civil Rights activists was, "If you're not part of the solution, you're part of the problem." The same could be said today by environmental activists, feminists, and others.) What good might come from your silence or refusal to take any action? What good might come from your responding assertively?

Defining the problem is an important first step in taking this kind of risk. The more clearly you understand the situation, the more deliberate and purposeful your action will be.

Examine Your Motivation

On examining your behavior in the hypothetical situation described above, one thing is obvious: you stood to gain very little by doing what you did. Your reason for speaking out had nothing to do with personal gain. On the contrary, you motivation was in large measure idealistic.

You can understand your motivation by clarifying your objective, and by getting in touch with the emotions that prompt your action. Clarify your objective by asking yourself what you hope to achieve by taking the risk. In the example, you wanted to heighten the checkout clerk's sensitivity to the fact that by telling "innocent" ethnic jokes, decent people promote prejudice and hurt others.

In addition to understanding your goals, examining your motivation means getting to the bottom of the emotions that spark your behavior. Sometimes this is easy, as in the example: you were offended by what you heard, but saw the occasion as an opportunity to teach an important lesson. On other occasions, it's more difficult to identify the emotional origins of your behavior. Skill in identifying them can be developed by getting into the habit of asking yourself two basic questions: "How do I feel right now?" and "What do I want?"

The more you know about your motivation, the more your actions will be deliberate and honest, and less likely to be encumbered by selfish or destructive impulses.

Weighing the Potential Negative Consequences of Your Action and Reducing Them to a Minimum

In the example, potential negative consequences were minimal, requiring no extraordinary consideration.

In other situations, potential negative consequences can be serious, even irreversible. When this is the case, it's essential that these consequences be examined; and you must make every effort to reduce them as much as possible.

Consider these examples:

- A gay person who comes out of the closet does so with full knowledge that her action may cause the loss of friends, a job, and more. Prudence dictates that some reasonable precautions be taken to avoid bringing unnecessary suffering upon herself.

- A demonstrator who joins a protest march through a hostile community must assess the dangers involved in marching, and make every effort to protect herself.

- A "whistle-blower" decides to contact her senator to report waste and mismanagement in a government-financed project being completed by the company she works for. Since she has a family to support, she must do all she can to ensure that she doesn't lose her job.

Anticipating, preventing, and preparing for potential negative consequences is the only rational course of action to take in cases like these.

Below is a worksheet you can use to prepare for risks of the type discussed here. Practice using it by thinking of some commitment or self-disclosure risks that you are considering taking. (Remember, your motivation should not involve an overt, practical, or personal benefit.) Respond to the questions in the spaces provided in Exercise 5.

Exercise 5: Preparing for Self-Disclosure and Commitment Risks Undertaken for Selfless or Idealistic Reasons

What is the problem, opportunity, or distressing situation that I'm responding to?

- Who is involved in this situation?

- How did the situation come about?

- In what ways might I respond to this situation, and how are my various responses likely to be interpreted?

What is my motivation for taking this risk?

- What do I hope to achieve by risking?

- Who will benefit from my risking? In what ways?

- What emotions or needs underlie my action?

What are the potential negative consequences of my risk?

- What can I do to reduce negative consequences to a minimum?

Self-Improvement Risks Without Tangible Benefits

Self-improvement risks that aren't intended to benefit you in some tangible way call for similar preparation. However, because they most often lack potential negative consequences, you usually have to replace questions about those outcomes with questions about how much of a sacrifice (inconvenience, expense, etc.) you're prepared to incur.

Suppose you want to learn to play the violin. You have no desire to become a professional musician, but simply want to develop your skill and deepen your appreciation of music. You can prepare for this kind of self-improvement risk by completing the following exercise:

Exercise 6: Preparing for Self-Improvement Risks Undertaken for No Tangible Benefit

What is the problem or opportunity I'm facing?

- Who else (if anyone) is involved in this situation?

- How did the problem or opportunity come about?

- In what ways might I respond?

What is my motivation for taking this risk?

- What do I hope to achieve by risking?

- What emotions or needs underlie my motivation?

What sacrifices am I willing to make to accomplish my goal?

- How much time am I willing to give?

- How much money am I willing to invest?

- How much effort am I willing to expend?

Tying It All Together

Beginning on the next page is a detailed, six-page questionnaire you can use to assess your risk readiness. Reproduce and use the questionnaire whenever you intend to take an important risk. This is a great way to ensure that your preparation has been as thoroughgoing as possible.

Although there are similarities in the way you prepare for all risk-taking, the specific preparation required depends on the outcome you seek. To prepare for risks involving a tangible benefit, follow Procedure One: define the problem clearly, set goals, analyze your risk, and conduct a "what-if" analysis. To prepare for risks that have no tangible benefit, follow Procedure Two: identify the problem, opportunity, or distressing situation you face; examine your motivation; identify the potential negative consequences of your action, and do all you can to reduce these to a minimum.

By using the Pre-Risk Questionnaire, you can maximize your readiness in any risky venture. In the next chapter, you'll learn the three stages of risking that follow preparation.

Pre-Risk Questionnaire

Description of the Risk To Be Taken

(Include what kind of risk this is: self-improvement, commitment, or self-disclosure?)

What makes this action risky for me? What am I putting on the line — my emotional or financial security? My career? A relationship I value?

Motivation

Is the risk I intend to take motivated by a feeling of dissatisfaction? If so, with what or whom am I dissatisfied? How strong is my dissatisfaction?

Is my risk motivated by something other than a feeling of dissatisfaction (for example, idealism, humanitarian motives)?

If I won't personally benefit from my risk-taking, who will? How?

Pre-Risk Questionnaire

page 2

Feelings

What feelings are triggered when I think about taking this risk? (For example, do I feel afraid, capable, excited)?

How strong are these feelings?

Why do I feel this way?

What will I do to cope with any negative feelings?

Overall Confidence Level

How confident do I feel?

If I'm not very confident, what would I need to do to build more confidence? Would I need to acquire specific skills, gather information, or consult with others who have taken this risk successfully?

Pre-Risk Questionnaire

page 3

Obstacles

What fears will influence whether or not I take this risk? *(See Chapter 4 for help in identifying the fears than can hold you back.)*

What will I do to cope with each fear? *(Review fear management techniques in Chapters 4, 5, and 6.)*

What other obstacles (for example, my upbringing, my past experiences) will influence whether or not I take this risk?

How can I overcome or minimize the effects of these obstacles?

Sacrifices Required

Am I aware of the sacrifices I have to make to take this risk? For example, will I have to give up immediate satisfactions for the sake of long-term ones? Will others be displeased because I choose to go ahead?

Pre-Risk Questionnaire

page 4

Have I decided how much time, money, effort, or other resources I'm willing to invest? (Explain.)

Problem Analysis

What is the problem, opportunity, or distressing situation?

What should be happening now that isn't?

What is actually happening now that shouldn't be happening?

What could be happening (in the best of all possible worlds)?

Pre-Risk Questionnaire

page 5

Who is part of this problem?

What are the key variables that have an impact on my taking this risk?

What would happen if I did nothing?

What's my estimate of the likelihood that I'll succeed? Are the odds acceptable?

What would I lose if I took this risk and failed totally?

What's my estimate of the likelihood of total failure? What about the likelihood of partial success? With what portion of success would I be satisfied?

What unavoidable negative consequences, if any, are associated with taking this risk?

Pre-Risk Questionnaire

page 6

What steps have I taken to reduce these consequences to a minimum?

What's my estimate of the probability of different problems and "glitches" I might encounter?

Do I have in mind a set of contingency plans for each potential problem? (Explain.)

Have I studied the timing of my risk? Am I satisfied that this is the best time to act? (Explain.)

If the outcome of my risk-taking depends on the goodwill or cooperation of others, do I have a good understanding of the people involved? Am I confident that I know how to work with them? (Explain.)

Have I considered and prepared for other variables that can influence my risk-taking? (Explain.)

8

Commitment, Guilt Management, Monitoring, and Evaluation

Once you've prepared for risk-taking and decided to go ahead, implementation is your next task. To carry out your risks successfully, it's necessary to do three things: (1) commit yourself, (2) manage any feelings of guilt, (3) monitor your progress, and (4) conduct a post-risk analysis.

Part One: Commit Yourself

Your risks can only succeed if you commit yourself to them. This means jumping in with both feet, wholly investing yourself in your decision to risk. Halfway measures are inappropriate at this point. Of course you should not be oblivious to the consequences of your risk-taking. Later in this chapter, you'll see that corrections in your course may be required, depending on your progress.

Committing yourself requires that you understand your risk and anticipate your feelings surrounding it.

Understanding Your Risk

The difficulty involved in making and maintaining a commitment varies by the kind of risk you're taking. Besides the other ways in which risks can be categorized by type, there are six dimensions that color the difficulty of making a commitment to a particular risk:

1. Risks vary according to whether they're quickly over or more drawn out.

2. Some risks provide immediate gratification; others require sustained effort over long periods of time, with little or no short-term payback.

3. Some risks have a low discouragement potential; others have a high one.

4. In some risks the stakes are low; in others the stakes are very high.

5. Risks vary in the extent to which they are reversible.

6. Risks vary by the likelihood of the desired payoff.

Each dimension has an impact on just how easy or hard it is to commit yourself to a given risk. These six dimensions are discussed in greater detail below.

1. Risks vary according to whether they're quickly over or more drawn out. Some risks are quickly over. Once a sky diver decides to jump, it takes only a second to jump out of the airplane. The crisis comes and goes quickly; and once the decision is made, there's no turning back. The sky diver very quickly passes the point of no return. Similarly, if you were house-hunting and were presented with a remarkable buying opportunity — perhaps a house you've been watching for several weeks has just been reduced by $30,000 — you would need to move quickly to make your bid. The "window of opportunity" for such a risk is very narrow; and once you make your decision (either by bidding or not bidding), the risk-taking opportunity is quickly over.

Other risks are more drawn out. They afford many opportunities to vacillate, hesitate, lose heart, and second-guess yourself. Elective surgery, for example, is always a difficult decision. Consider, also, the case of Jeremy, who decided to submit his artwork to a juried show. At every point in the process, Jeremy found himself vacillating. He took a long time to complete the required papers. He could not easily decide which works to submit. He agonized over shipping arrangements.

An adult who decides to return to college can also lose heart at many of the points along the way: requesting an application, completing it, arranging for letters of recommendation and other supporting materials, accepting the offer of admission, sending in the required deposit, registering for classes, attending classes, and so on.

If your risk is drawn out, you must make a special effort to keep your goal in mind throughout the process. Never lose sight of what you're trying to accomplish. The greater the number of steps you must take before finally arriving at your destination, the greater the danger that your commitment will waver.

2. Some risks provide immediate gratification; others require sustained effort over long periods of time, with little or no short-term payoff. The outcomes of some choices are experienced quickly. They require a minimal personal investment; your actions are rewarded with an almost immediate payoff. For example, when you choose one TV show over another, you usually know right away whether you've made the right choice. After investing a few minutes of your time, you can easily make a decision about whether to stay tuned.

The same is true about buying an article of clothing (so long as you can afford to make the purchase). You know right away whether you made the right choice by noticing how you look in the mirror and the reactions of others.

Some risks, on the other hand, require extraordinary patience. Gratification is far from immediate; in fact, you may not know for a long time whether your risk will pay off at all. It may take years before the fruits of your labor are enjoyed. The rewards that come from attending college, professional or graduate school, for example, may not be experienced for many years. It takes a special kind of discipline to persist under such circumstances. The same can be said about learning to play a musical instrument or studying a very difficult foreign language. This principle applies to a wide range of risks, from planting an orchard to investing in the stock of a "turnaround" company.

In all these cases, the payoff is long-term and gratification must be postponed. To resist wavering in your commitment, you must keep your goal in mind and bolster your self-confidence. Reassure yourself that one day you will enjoy the fruits of your investment.

3. Some risks have a low discouragement potential; others have a high one. When automotive engineers introduced the automatic transmission, they eliminated a major difficulty new drivers faced: learning to change gears by using the clutch and gear-shift lever. People who might have been daunted by the difficulty of learning to drive were suddenly able to take command of a car.

Similar developments have occurred in education (the hand-held calculator has eliminated the need to learn certain mathematical functions), cooking (convenience foods and microwave ovens have made it possible for even children to provide their own meals), and many other activities. In such cases, the emphasis has been on making things easy, reducing or eliminating the opportunities for discouragement or outright failure.

Such developments have reduced the anxiety and uncertainty associated with taking certain risks, greatly reducing their discouragement potential.

But there are other risks that no amount of technological innovation can ever render discouragement-proof. These are accompanied by countless opportunities to lose heart.

Risks involving particular skills require that you learn by doing; making errors is part of the learning process. You can only achieve mastery in skiing, painting, competitive cycling, piano, and similar skills by learning from your mistakes.

The other class of risks with a high discouragement potential is called "nonreductive." Unlike skill-building, where your odds for success increase with practice, the chances for success in nonreductive risks do not improve over time. The odds of your succeeding or failing remain the same each time you repeat your risk. For example, each time you play the state lottery, your chances of winning are basically the same as the last time you played.

There are two strategies you can use to help you remain committed to a risk with a high discouragement potential. The first is to keep your goal in mind. The second is to keep track of your progress. This is particularly important when you are learning a skill. You will see incremental improvement as you work and practice. Acknowledging this progress, however slight, will help keep you from wavering in your commitment.

4. In some risks the stakes are low; in others the stakes are very high. Some risks require that you put very little on the line. For example, suppose you know of two restaurants that have recently opened in your neighborhood. Unless one has a particular history of food poison, the choice of which to eat in is a low-stakes risk. The same is true of choosing among consumer items. When you choose one brand of laundry detergent over another, the stakes are ordinarily very low.

It's much more difficult to commit yourself to risks that have higher stakes. These include deciding which car to buy, putting a deposit on a home, or choosing one career over another. What makes these stakes so high is not just the dollar value of what you're choosing (to a poor person, buying a $500 car might be a high-stakes risk), but the fact that you'll probably live with the consequences of your choice for a long time.

The risks with the highest stakes are formative life choices whose implications are far-reaching. The decision to marry is one such risk. So is the decision to have a child.

The higher the stakes involved in your risking, the more careful and thorough your preparation must be. However, once you've made such a decision, it's essential that you commit yourself 100 percent. (Indeed, that's why the institutions of society have long tended to make it difficult for people to change their mind about serious commitments. Not until this century, for example, has it been relatively easy to obtain a divorce.)

5. Risks vary in the extent to which they are reversible. Most risks can be seen as falling along a continuum of permanence. At one end are the easily reversible risks. Buying an item from a retailer with a liberal return policy is a good example of such a risk. When you know there's a "30-day satisfaction guarantee," and that you can return an item, "no questions asked," there's not much reason to hesitate about making the purchase.

A middle group of risks are reversible, too; but more time is required before things can be put back to rights. For example, when you have your hair cut and styled in a dramatic new way, you know it's not forever; nevertheless, if you discover that you hate the way you look, you might have to wait a while before your hair grows out again. This is a category of risks often taken by teenagers who want to make a statement, but have the inherent good sense not to disfigure themselves in any permanent way: weird hairdos are transitory, and even pierced skin will eventually grow back together.

At the other extreme are the risks that are reversible only at the great risk of inconvenience — or not at all. Buying an expensive stereo system from a store that's going out of business is an example. More serious ones include having a child and having irreversible surgery, such as a hysterectomy or donating a kidney.

6. Risks vary by the likelihood of their desired payoff. Some risks offer a very high likelihood of success. If an investor puts her money into a large company with a long history of steady earnings, the odds are that she'll make money. Her profits might not be dramatic, but the risk of loss is relatively low.

On the other hand, investing in an emerging growth company with a short but spectacular earnings history may result in substantial profit. However, the payoff is extremely uncertain.

The higher your probability of success, the lower your anxiety and ambivalence are likely to be. The lower your odds of succeeding, the higher your level of courage and tenaciousness must be.

The Commitment Coefficient

In implementing any risk, it's useful to assess how easy or difficult it will be to commit yourself to your choice. By evaluating your risk along the six dimensions discussed, you'll be able to make that assessment and gear yourself up to the proper degree.

A commitment coefficient — a numerical measure of just how easy or how difficult it will be to commit yourself to a given risk — can be calculated for every risk you contemplate. You can make this calculation by rating a risk in terms of the dimensions described above.

The following worksheet reduces these dimensions to a series of six graduated scales.

Make a photocopy of the entire worksheet. Then use it for a particular risk you're contemplating. Rate the risk along each of the scales in the worksheet. Then total up your score and enter it in the space at the bottom.

The example that follows the blank worksheet will help you understand the scoring process.

152

Commitment Coefficient Worksheet

Risk I want to take:_____

Mark each scale at the point that best describes your planned risk.
Characteristics of the Risk:

/_____/_____/_____/_____/_____/_____/_____/
    -3   -2   -1   0   +1   +2   +3

quickly over   **Speed of completion**   drawn out

/_____/_____/_____/_____/_____/_____/_____/
    -3   -2   -1   0   +1   +2   +3

immediate   **Speed of gratification**   remote

/_____/_____/_____/_____/_____/_____/_____/
    -3   -2   -1   0   +1   +2   +3

few   **Opportunities for discouragement**   many

/_____/_____/_____/_____/_____/_____/_____/
    -3   -2   -1   0   +1   +2   +3

low   **Stakes**   high

/_____/_____/_____/_____/_____/_____/_____/
    -3   -2   -1   0   +1   +2   +3

highly   **Reversibility**   not at all

/_____/_____/_____/_____/_____/_____/_____/
    -3   -2   -1   0   +1   +2   +3

very high   **Likelihood of desired payoff**   none

Sum of scores:		If your commitment coefficient is	...you'll find commitment to be
Speed of completion	____	-18 to -6	a piece of cake
Speed of gratification	____	-5 to 0	fairly easy
Opportunity for discouragement	____	+1 to +6	problematic
Stakes	____	+7 to +18	extremely difficult
Reversibility	____		
Likelihood of desired payoff	____		
Commitment Coefficient =	____		

Commitment Coefficient Worksheet

Risk I want to take: *enroll in a six-week course to prepare for the state real estate license exam*

Mark each scale at the point that best describes your planned risk.
Characteristics of the Risk:

```
/____/_x_/____/____/____/____/____/
 -3   -2   -1    0   +1   +2   +3
```
quickly over　　　**Speed of completion**　　　drawn out

```
/____/____/____/____/_x_/____/____/
 -3   -2   -1    0   +1   +2   +3
```
immediate　　　**Speed of gratification**　　　remote

```
/____/____/_x_/____/____/____/____/
 -3   -2   -1    0   +1   +2   +3
```
few　　　**Opportunities for discouragement**　　　many

```
/____/_x_/____/____/____/____/____/
 -3   -2   -1    0   +1   +2   +3
```
low　　　**Stakes**　　　high

```
/_x_/____/____/____/____/____/____/
 -3   -2   -1    0   +1   +2   +3
```
highly　　　**Reversibility**　　　not at all

```
/_x_/____/____/____/____/____/____/
 -3   -2   -1    0   +1   +2   +3
```
very high　　　**Likelihood of desired payoff**　　　none

Sum of scores:		*If your commitment coefficient is...*	*it will be...*
Speed of completion	-2	-18 to -6	a piece of cake
Speed of gratification	+1	-5 to 0	fairly easy
Opportunities for discouragement	-1	+1 to +6	problematic
Stakes	-2	+7 to +18	extremely difficult
Reversibility	-3		
Payoff	+3		
Commitment Coefficient =	-4		

How To Implement a Risk With a High Commitment Coefficient

If a risk you're planning to take has a high commitment coefficient, you'll need to work hard to keep yourself focused, optimistic, and invested emotionally. Generally, the higher the coefficient, the more headwork you'll need to do before and during your risk-taking. Here are several suggestions for maintaining your commitment.

Keep your goal in mind. Although we've said this before, the point bears repeating. Write down your goal on an index card. Post it in your car, or put in a prominent place at home where you'll see it every day. Refer to your written reminder often.

It's just as easy to lose focus as to lose motivation. One key to remaining committed is to stay on track. Rather than running off in many directions, once you've set your mind on a task, don't allow yourself to be diverted. One of the hallmarks of successful and effective people is that they know what they're trying to accomplish; and they steer clear of distractions that might keep them from reaching their goal.

Divide your task into increments and give yourself rewards along the way. For example, one amateur pianist with a love of Chopin set himself the task of learning a long and complex piece of music. Knowing that it would take several months to learn, he analyzed it in terms of how it might be divided into parts. Then he set out to master each part. He simplified his task still further, deciding first to learn one hand, then the other, for each part. Each time he mastered one hand in each part, he gave himself a treat: dinner out with his wife, a book he wanted to buy, and so on. (Of course the pleasure of listening to the music he made was, to a very great degree, its own reward.)

Be kind to yourself. Lapses of motivation are normal for most people who are pursuing long-range goals. Discouragement is common. When letdowns occur, accept them as temporary states triggered by physical fatigue, mental weariness, or other factors. Rather than denying these feelings, accept them. Rest. Take a break from your routine. And remind yourself that a good night's sleep, a good meal, or a change of scenery will do much to improve your spirits.

Emotional factors play a major role in activities that require maintaining a commitment over long periods of time. The emotional component in committing yourself to your risks is the focus of the next section of this chapter.

Avoid sending yourself messages that are likely to increase your discomfort. Cognitive distortions — or wrong-headed thinking — can undermine the commitment and discipline required to succeed at any task with a high commitment coefficient. By aggressively ferreting out negative self-talk, you'll go a long way toward preparing your-self to hang in there for the long haul.

Reassurance builds confidence. The nice thing is that you can offer yourself needed reassurance whenever and wherever you need it.

Anticipate feelings. In committing yourself to your risk, it's essential to know not only its commitment coefficient, but also to anticipate the feelings it's likely to engender. This increases the likelihood that you won't be "thrown" by them; anticipating feelings enables you to prepare yourself for them.

The two feelings you are most likely to experience as a risk-taker, and two which are most likely to cause you trouble, are anxiety and guilt. To some degree or other, all risks evoke these feelings. But psychological risks are especially likely to trigger them.

Refer back to Chapter 6 for techniques for mastering your anxiety. The section that follows deals with feelings of guilt and how to cope with them.

Guilt

Feelings of guilt almost always accompany risks, particularly those that involve your identity, or self-image. To risk successfully, you have to learn to manage your guilt and persist in spite of it. This section of the chapter touches upon what guilt is, why psycho-logical risking inspires it, and how to respond constructively to it.

What Guilt Is

Most people in our culture have an instinctive grasp of what guilt is. In short, it's a feeling of having done something wrong (or not having done something you feel you should have done). You feel guilty when you believe that you have violated some law or failed to live up to a standard, whether internal or external. You feel guilty when you think you've displeased a person whose judgment counts in your eyes.

Guilt can be induced by others, as when a parent puts a "guilt trip" on a child ("go ahead and treat me like a dog — I'm only your mother!"); or it can be self-imposed. You make yourself feel guilty when you label or victimize yourself by means of *should* state-ments. For example, you may label yourself selfish for wanting to invest money in an elaborate exercise machine or wanting to take an expensive self-improvement course. You may also feel guilty when you want something you feel you "shouldn't" want, such as an opportunity to go away with friends over a holiday instead of spending it with your family.

Guilt and Psychological Risks

Why does guilt accompany almost all the risks that serve to define you as an individual? The reason can be traced back to a contradiction that is inherent in human nature. On the one hand, you're driven toward adventure, growth, and self-expansion. But you're also inclined to cling to the safe, secure, and familiar. No one can move forward without leaving something — or someone — behind. You can't grow without turning your back, to some degree, on what you have known and been.

You know that your leaving others behind will disappoint and upset them; perhaps they will even feel betrayed. Because of this realization, you are bound to feel guilty. This is a universal experience shared by people as they venture toward maturity. (The biblical tale of Adam and Eve shows that a guilty and fearful regret accompanies each of our decisions to grow, for with every one we move farther from the innocence and lack of self-consciousness that characterize youth.)

Your guilty feelings are almost always heightened by the reactions of those around you. All human groups are systemic. They tend to establish and maintain the balance that's essential to their survival, just as, for example, your body's temperature-control mechanisms work together to keep your temperature close to 98.6.

When one member of a family or friendship group begins changing and growing, he or she threatens to upset the balance that has enabled the system to survive. An automatic response on the part of others is to discourage that change, since it threatens the system. "Change back!" is the message typically sent to the person whose behavior is threatening. Frequently this takes the form of a guilt induction. Thus, the mother who seeks to discourage a child from leaving home might say, "I don't know how I'll manage without your help." Her real message is a plea to the child not to upset the family balance — and not to change.

Another reason why guilt accompanies psychological risks is that destruction accompanies every act of creation. The colonies that became the United States of America had to break their ties with Great Britain in order to give birth to a new nation. A sculptor must destroy a piece of marble to make a statue. In the same way, you must destroy what you've been in order to become what you're capable of becoming.

How To Manage Guilt

Guilt can stop you from committing yourself to your risks. To keep it in check, use the two strategies detailed below.

Guilt that's imposed by others. Don't allow yourself to buy into manipulation by others. Recognize "Change back!" messages for what they are. And remind yourself that you have the right to persist in your risk, whether your goal is to develop yourself (as in self-improvement risks), to speak your mind (as in self-disclosure risks), or to put yourself on the line for your convictions (as in commitment risks).

Often, "Change back!" messages are designed to manipulate by inducing guilt. Everyone is guilty of this type of manipulation at one time or another, some because they themselves have so little feeling of control in their lives. Manipulators typically don't assume responsibility for the subjective nature of their feelings. Instead, they behave as though they were the mouthpiece for eternal and universal truths. For example, a manipulative spouse will not say, "I want you to come with me when I visit my parents" (which would be an assertive statement, since the speaker acknowledges subjective needs). Instead, he or she will say, "You should come with me to my parents," or "If you loved me, you'd visit my family," or, worse still, "You should want to visit my parents!"

When you realize that such assertions are nothing more than disguised statements of personal preference, it's easier to see that they do not capture eternal truths nor state principles that are beyond discussion. You don't need to feel guilty because you don't want what another person wants you to want.

There are a number of ways of responding to such manipulation. If your goal is simply to bring the manipulation to a halt, agree with the critic, but persist in doing what you want. The dialogue below shows what we mean.

Manipulator: You should want to visit my parents.

You: Perhaps I should, but I don't.

Manipulator: That sounds selfish to me.

You: Yes, I guess it is selfish.

Manipulator: Well, don't you feel bad? Don't you have any shame?

You: I guess I have no shame at all.

No matter what the manipulator says, you stop the manipulation dead by agreeing in principle with the guilt-inculcating statement.

If you value the relationship and want to make good communication possible, you may want to promote discussion (and not simply blunt the manipulative criticism). When that's your intent, use a technique that draws the other person out. This is called *negative inquiry*. Ask what it is about your behavior that's upsetting. The question forces the manipulator to clarify the personal, subjective basis for the criticism. That makes open discussion possible.

Manipulator: You should want to visit my parents.

You: What is it about my not wanting to visit your parents that's upsetting to you?

The question forces the manipulator to clarify the personal, subjective basis for his or her criticism. That makes open discussion possible.

Guilt that's self-induced. Purge yourself of the tendency to induce guilt in yourself. There are six logical fallacies that most commonly result in guilt feelings: should statements, labeling, emotional reasoning, catastrophizing, personalization, and filtering. (For help in recognizing these, review the section on cognitive distortions in Chapter 6.)

Productive Responses to Guilt

Typical nonproductive responses to guilt include quitting (abandoning your dreams or giving up on whatever it is you're doing that's evoking the displeasure of others), punishing yourself, and falling into the victim role, which causes you to resent the people who "hold you back" or "make you do things." Some people live their entire lives walking the narrow line between guilt and resentment — an unhappy existence, indeed!

One productive and mature way to respond to guilt imposed by others is to let them know that while you appreciate their wants and feelings, you must respect your own as well. Furthermore, you plan to hearken to your wants and feelings in determining your future.

But be careful. There is a narrow line between offering understanding on the one hand, and "explaining" yourself and perhaps backing down on the other. Don't lose sight of the fact that sensitivity to someone's feelings is not the same as responsibility for them.

Try to accept guilt as a necessary part of growth. Only sociopaths are capable of living guilt-free: a certain amount of guilt helps motivate people to follow the rules that keep society running smoothly. Guilt is only a problem when it's unreasoned or out of proportion to the actions or circumstances involved.

Don't do anything you don't want to do. Although this prescription may sound like an open invitation to irresponsibility, its real meaning is that good results usually come from acts that are performed willingly and wholeheartedly. Rather than allowing yourself to feel coerced into behaving a particular way, affirm your choices with the dictates of your heart.

Part Two: Monitor Your Risk

Anxiety and guilt can interfere unreasonably with committing yourself to a risk. But blind commitment can also be a mistake. Although it's important to commit yourself and "dive in" when you take a risk, you must also keep track of your progress and gauge the effectiveness and efficiency of your risk-taking.

Robert and Jeanette Lauer, in *Watersheds*, advise their readers to "persevere within reason." Persistence, they say, is almost always a key to success in any endeavor. What's more, patience and perseverance can pay off handsomely. On the other hand, the Lauers caution that perseverance can be foolhardy when there is absolutely no hope of success.

You are left, then, asking yourself how to determine whether your risk-taking is succeeding. How do you know when to quit? When should you change course? Fortunately, there are several methodical ways of addressing these questions.

Risks With Overt Outcomes

If your risks are taken to achieve some external, measurable outcome, ask yourself: Are my actions bringing me closer to my goal? Are the costs commensurate with the possible benefits? If my risks are inefficient, how can I use my time, energy, and resources more wisely? Can I use back-up strategies that can help me reach my goal more quickly and efficiently?

For example, if you risk money, energy, and time to launch a business, you can determine effectiveness by measuring how quickly your sales are increasing. You can keep track of how much profit you're making. And you can use other objective tests of business success.

If you risk time and energy in preparing for a test, you can measure the effectiveness of your risk in the grade you receive.

If you invest energy in pursuing a relationship, you can measure your success by whether he or she responds positively.

If you're trying a new teaching strategy, you can measure whether your students are doing better.

Risks Without Overt Outcomes

When your goal is internal — personal growth, increased self-esteem, and so on — the payoff is less easily measurable. You must do without objective or tangible yardsticks. In cases like these, your risk must be its own reward. It would be a grave error to attempt to measure the effectiveness of your risk-taking by looking for signs of change in your environment. What you may see are changes in your feelings about yourself, or changes in the way other people relate to you; but such changes are pretty hard to measure.

This principle applies to all three types of psychological risks. For example, if you commit yourself to helping the poor and the downtrodden, the effectiveness of your risk-taking can't always be determined by gauging the impact of your actions on one particular person or on one particular community of people. Your most tangible indicator may be the feeling of fulfillment that comes from simply trying to help.

The law enforcement officer or member of the criminal justice system who makes a commitment to the maintenance of law and order can't evaluate his or her success in terms of whether or not crime is reduced. The real reward in doing such work is internal: living up to one's own standards and values. If, at the same time, crime is reduced and wrong-doers are punished for their crimes, so much the better. But to use crime statistics as a measure of effectiveness is to invite frustration and feelings of failure.

If you take the self-disclosure risk of confronting someone who is exploiting you, that person's response would not be a reliable measure of the success of your risk. If the exploitation stops and the relationship improves, so much the better. But if that doesn't happen, that's no indication that you've failed. You've succeeded by virtue of having risked the confrontation. (If your goal was to stop the exploitation and maintain the relationship, then total success requires that you accomplish both purposes. Reality, however, often demands compromises. For many people, stopping the exploitation — even at the expense of the relationship — would constitute a success.)

Many self-fulfillment risks are taken because you wish to enrich your life in some way rather than for practical purposes. The amateur voice student, archaeologist, or gardener would certainly be pleased if the results of his or her efforts were praiseworthy. But the sort of success that engenders praise should be regarded as a mere fringe benefit. The real purpose of such risking is to deepen your understanding and appreciation of the subject you study. Once again, your risk provides its own reward.

Knowing When To Bail Out

There are situations in which you must be willing to reconsider your decisions. To plunge ahead when there's no reason to expect things to get better is foolish in the extreme.

Take the example of Cory, who went to work as the only nonfamily member in a family-owned business. Eager to prove herself and very talented, Cory put in long hours. She brought to the company creativity and talent that no family member had ever shown. She believed that she would be rewarded for her very substantial contributions; hence, she was willing to risk investing a great deal of time, energy, and effort. Nevertheless, because she was an outsider, nothing she did brought her the advancement she had hoped for. Despite her high hopes, it became apparent after several months that she would never break through the inner circle. Cory knew that it was time to bail out.

Marla took an elective English course in college because she was sincerely interested in the subject matter and wanted to improve her writing. Enthusiastic and eager to learn, she put aside the misgivings that crossed her mind on the first day of class when the professor struck her as a bit standoffish and uninspired. "Perhaps he's having a bad day," she said to herself. Unfortunately, his bad day lasted for most of the semester. Nothing Marla did could satisfy this man. In his eyes, her writing style was "immature," and her class participation was "below par." Unfortunately, Marla let too many weeks go by before making the decision to withdraw from the course. If she dropped out, she would receive an automatic F. Wisely, therefore, she elected not to withdraw. However, to spare herself frustration and damage to her self-esteem, she bailed out emotionally. She went through the motions of taking the class, but no longer invested herself psychologically. She completed all the readings; she submitted the required work. Her expectations dropped sharply, insulating her from this negative, unenthusiastic teacher.

As these two examples show, there's more than one way to abandon ship when it's clear that perseverence won't pay off. Sometimes it's possible to leave the situation entirely. At other times you must find a way to remain in the situation but hold back emotionally so that you're no more vulnerable than you need to be.

The following questionnaire can guide you in making the decision about whether to quit or continue. Make a photocopy of the questionnaire so that you can use it more than once.

Questionnaire:
When To Bail Out

1. Before risking, did I place limits on the amount of time, energy, and effort I would invest in attempting to reach my goal? Have I met or exceeded those limits?

2. What's the probability that I'll achieve my goal if I persevere? (If this is difficult to estimate, discuss possible scenarios and your best guess at their likelihood.)

3. Do I have any logical reason to believe that my goal is attainable? (Explain.)

4. What would have to happen for me to succeed? How likely is it that this will come about?

   - What people would have to change for me to succeed? How likely is it that they will?

   - What circumstances would have to change for me to succeed? How likely is it that they will?

Questionnaire:
When To Bail Out

page 2

5. Am I persevering more out of habit and blind hope than with thought-fullness, deliberateness, and a reasonable expectation of success? (Explain.)

6. Is there anything on the horizon that might influence my situation and improve the likelihood that I'll achieve my goal?

7. Can I estimate realistically how long it will take me to reach my goal? If not, is it reasonable to continue? If I can estimate the amount of time required, is that time frame acceptable?

8. To what extent is the achievement of my goal in my own hands? If not entirely, what factors will influence the outcome of my risk? To what degree can I predict or influence their contribution to my success?

Part Three: Conduct a Post-Risk Analysis

Once you've taken a risk, you can learn a great deal and also benefit emotionally by reviewing your experience. There are four principles that can guide you in retrospectively evaluating a risky venture.

Principle 1: Only You Can Judge the Outcome of Your Risk

One of the most insidious things that children learn is that the worth of their efforts is relative. They learn early, both at home and at school, that their success will be compared with that of others. Hence, they often find themselves in competition not only with themselves but with children who may be more developmentally advanced or talented.

Second, they learn that others — such as parents and teachers — have the right to judge their behavior, thoughts, and actions. Of course, children lack worldly experience and so need the guidance that responsible adults can provide. The problem is that some adults overstep their bounds. Conditioned to advising, judging, and prescribing, they may not know when to stop. Even well-meaning adults may deny children the valuable experience of making choices and judgments, and learning for themselves. This can have serious repercussions when the child becomes an adult.

For many people, the experience of being judged for so many years results in their becoming adults who remain too eager to please and be accepted. They surrender to others the right to judge them long after they have developed the capacity to judge things for themselves.

One of the most valuable lessons you can learn from this book is that you have the right to judge yourself. Applied to evaluating your risk-taking, this means that nobody but you can judge the worth of your risks.

When Betty left graduate school to open her own flower shop, she invested enormous amounts of time and most of her savings to make it work. But the economy was poor, competition was stiff, and Betty's business failed. Her family and acquaintances, quick to find fault, criticized her for leaving school and then making poor business decisions. But Betty didn't share their harsh judgment of her. "I made some mistakes," she said. "That's what life's about. I'm young. I can try again. I learned a lot and grew up. Next time, I'll get it right!" Her response was a healthy, adult one. She refused to accept the fault-finding of others. Instead, she correctly made her own judgment about her experience.

Principle 2: Respond to Success Constructively

A constructive response to success requires that you take pleasure in your accomplishments. There is a basic principle in psychology: behavior that is reinforced positively tends to be repeated. For the risk-taker, this means that your successful risk-taking is more likely to be repeated if you savor your success.

Not only can you profit by enjoying your success, the people around you can, too. Vince was an ambitious, intelligent man with a clear sense of purpose. A teacher and father of two, he decided early in his career that he would become an educational administrator. This, he knew, would take several years of graduate courses. Vince became so programmed to accomplish his goals that he forgot to enjoy his work, life, wife, and children. Almost every time he accomplished a difficult task, he went on to the next one without relishing his success. When he completed his Master's program, he never even thought seriously about attending the commencement ceremony. So far as he was concerned, his completion of the program was simply one more step toward his certification as an administrator. Vince failed to consider his wife's feelings in the matter. "I worked hard, too," she finally told him. "All those night courses, leaving me with the kids so often. I didn't mind it, Vince — but now I want to celebrate with you; to celebrate what we've both accomplished!"

You can only learn from success if you don't take it for granted. Review what you did to bring it about. This isn't smugness or an excess of self-satisfaction: if you know the steps you took, the pitfalls you avoided, the words you used to encourage yourself, you'll be able to make this journey again and again.

One of the most useful ways of accounting for your success is to take stock of the strengths and behaviors that made it possible. Ask yourself: What particular strengths of character or mind did I draw on in bringing about this success? Was I courageous when my nerves might have failed? Did I persevere when I might have become discouraged? Was I particularly good at planning and anticipating? Did I display unusual self-discipline or skill in time management?

In general, your purpose in analysing your success is to answer the question: What rules and guidelines can I apply to my next risk?

Principle 3: Respond to Failure Constructively

The same question applies when you've failed in your risk-taking: What lessons have I learned and how can I apply them to my next risk?

To answer this question after you've taken an unsuccessful risk means doing two things. First, admit your errors. Don't make the mistake of denying your part in the failure. Don't pretend that failing doesn't matter to you. Instead, look squarely at what you have done or failed to do that accounts for your not succeeding. Were you frightened when you might have been courageous? Did you become discouraged when you might have persevered? Did you fail to plan and anticipate? Did you display a lack of self-discipline or skill in time management?

On the other hand, don't make the mistake of beating up on yourself for your failures and errors. There's nothing constructive about torturing yourself by labeling ("I'm just a jerk"), overgeneralizing ("I'll never amount to anything"), fortune-telling ("Nobody will hire me now"), or engaging in other types of self-defeating thinking.

Finally, don't wallow in regret. Put past failures behind you and go on. The most constructive response to failure, or wrongdoing of any kind, is simply to get back on track.

Principle 4: Be Prepared for a Letdown

Whether you succeed or fail, when your risk-taking is over, you're likely to experience feelings of purposelessness, emptiness, or mild depression; after all, you've invested a lot in your risk-taking. The bigger the risk, the greater the letdown. The challenge you've met or tried to meet may have provided a focus in your life that you lacked before. To have come to an end is really to lose an organizing force in your life.

Preparing yourself for the letdown takes the sting out of it. Accept your feelings. Then slowly, without rushing or pushing yourself in any way, begin thinking about and planning your next risk.

Summary

In this chapter, you've seen what's required to implement your risks and make the most of them, regardless of whether your efforts succeed or fail.

Making a commitment to your risk-taking is essential, as is coping with the anxiety and guilt your experience engenders. It's necessary to monitor your risking and to evaluate it when it's all over.

The techniques, worksheets, and questionnaires throughout this chapter can help you accomplish each of these important tasks.

Further Reading

Lauer, R., and J. Lauer. (1988) *Watersheds*. Boston: Little, Brown, and Company.
Smith, M. (1975) *When I Say No I Feel Guilty*. New York: The Dial Press.

9

Helping Children
Learn to Take Risks

People who have learned to risk wisely and responsibly display many desirable characteristics. They know how to make decisions. They show initiative. They take responsibility for their choices. They are able to examine their behavior, accurately assess their environment, and formulate their own guidelines for a full and happy life.

Since these traits define a well-functioning human being, they have value at all stages of life and across a wide variety of activities. Children who know how to risk display age-appropriate independence. Within the limits imposed by their age and experience, they make sound judgments and know what it means to be responsible. As they grow older, they become active learners, inquisitive and goal-directed. They are also creative, innovative, and open to change.

If you are a parent, you will almost certainly want to encourage your children to risk wisely and responsibly. In this chapter you'll learn how.

Parenting To Prepare for Risk-Taking

Growth and risk are inseparable. This is particularly true for children, who must take many risks daily. They risk emotionally when they trust caregivers. They risk physically when they learn to stand, walk, and run.

Virtually all risking in childhood yields fruit, because there is so much to learn, and risking is part of the learning process. Thoughtful, goal-oriented risk-taking, however, develops over time.

The process by which children learn to take purposeful and psychologically meaningful risks is not entirely automatic. As a parent, you play a crucial role in cultivating your child's innate impulse to risk. In fulfilling that role, you give your child opportunities to make age-appropriate choices, you serve as a role model for mature risk-taking, and you help your child complete the process of self-definition.

Age-Appropriate Choices

Age-appropriate choices are risks that are suited to a child's physical maturity, judgment, and emotional development. For example:

- You let your toddler choose between favorite stuffed toys at bedtime.

- When your child is old enough to know which foods appeal to her, you allow her reasonable choices.

- You allow your three-year-old to dress himself.

- A five-or six-year-old might be allowed to choose a playmate to spend the night.

- A fourth-grader can be given the choice of whether to join a soccer league.

In all these cases, the risks permitted the child are tied to physical and emotional maturity. By gradually relaxing the rules regulating a youngster's behavior, and by increasing the responsibility she is allowed to assume, you show faith in your child and nurture her expanding capacities.

Each of us begins life by abiding by rules that exist outside ourselves. The two-year-old reaches for a hot pan on the stove; his mother slaps his hand and says, "No!" If he could put his feelings into words, he might say, "I want to touch that, and she won't let me!" The youngster relives this experience many times. As a primary school student, he calls out from the classroom to a friend passing in the hall. The teacher reprimands him.

His account of the event might be summarized in these words: "I want to be able to talk to my friends, and he won't let me." In his early teens, he wants to drive a car and learns that the state won't allow him to. He says to himself, "I want to drive, but the state won't let me."

If a youngster is to mature, external rules must be relaxed over time, and behavior must come to be regulated from within. This happens when children are raised in an atmosphere of concerned trust. They are allowed gradually to extend their area of free-dom. The loving and astute parent (or other adult authority) trusts them to take risks and to venture out independently. Slowly they develop capacities to make decisions and assume responsibility, becoming adept at self-directed behavior.

If children are denied the chance to make choices and learn from the consequences of poor decisions, they never develop internal behavioral controls. They may become resentful of authority. Rules and discipline become the source of pain and guilt. Perhaps most important, restrictions become entrenched in their minds as something clearly ex-ternal to themselves. They experience a lifelong tension between what they should do and what they want to do. They never learn to trust themselves, and instead become locked in a struggle between internal impulses and external restrictions.

While it's often easy to create opportunities for children to make their own choices, there are several reasons why many parents fail to do so.

First, it's not always easy or convenient to involve children in decision-making. The preschooler who wants to dress herself may choose clothing that's inappropriate for the weather. Or she may pick the worst possible moment to insist on choosing her clothes. For example, she may make her wishes known on a busy weekday morning, when her single parent is running late and must feed her, drop her off at the daycare center, and still get to work on time. Under ideal circumstances, the parent might take out a few different outfits, and permit the child to select one. But the process is time-consuming and requires a lot of patience. And when time is short, it's just not possible. (By the way, no great harm would be done, in the example cited, by denying the child a chance to choose. At some time in the future, the mother can invite the youngster to pick out her clothes for the day.)

Second, baggage from the parent's own childhood may interfere. One mother and daughter were locked in a struggle over the way the daughter cared for her bedroom. A rumpled bedspread or a casually thrown sweater was enough to spark a long and heated argument.

Discussion revealed that the mother had grown up in a three-room apartment with her mother and four brothers. Their living room was used as a bedroom, and had to be transformed into a meticulously neat and anonymous place every morning.

Three decades later, the woman lived with her family in a spacious home with ample bedrooms to ensure everyone's personal privacy. Had she wanted to, she could have shut the door to her daughter's room and left it closed. But because she was living by rules that were relevant to her circumstances 30 years ago, she failed to see that a little disorder in her daughter's room posed no threat or inconvenience for the rest of the family.

Third, parents may be reluctant to surrender the pleasures associated with caring for children and exercising control. It's nice to have someone around who really needs you; and it's pleasant to have things go just your way. But there's a danger in being unwilling to let go. If you consciously or unconsciously sabotage your child's initiative, you create a climate of fear in which the child never learns to gain a sure and independent footing.

Finally, a parent's own insecurities may interfere with giving children appropriate choices. The father who felt the lack of friends during childhood may get overly involved in managing his child's social life. The mother who had parents who were remote and uninvolved may make too many decisions for her youngsters. While in the short term such over-functioning parents may appear to be helpful, they can undermine their youngsters' ability to function independently. Secure parents can tolerate seeing their youngsters experience a little pain and discomfort. Recognizing that all growth and learning are accompanied by some distress, they resist the impulse to overfacilitate. They are there when needed, but they do not intrude.

Model Risk-Taking

Do you set goals? Make plans to reach them? Take calculated risks to carry them out? If you do, you've already taught your youngsters valuable lessons about self-improvement risks. By your model, your children have learned that it's good to aspire, and that achieving goals takes time, planning, and effort. Too often, children see media celebrities rise to stardom seemingly overnight. Pop heroes earn huge salaries for what seems like little exertion. Through your own hard work and thoughtful risking, you can help shatter the myths of easy success: that good things come to those who sit and wait, and that there is such a thing as instant gratification.

Do you commit yourself to values that are important to you? For example, are you involved in your community and willing to invest time and other resources in significant issues? If so, your children have already learned that there's value in taking commitment risks.

In your day-to-day dealings with others, do you take self-disclosure risks? It may seem surprising, but youngsters learn the most about risk-taking by observing the way in which you communicate with them and others. They hear how you exercise authority, how you offer praise and criticism, how you negotiate disagreements, and how you express your feelings. All these things shape their attitudes toward risk-taking.

Assertive Exercise of Authority

When you behave in an assertive way, you model directness and openness. By manipulating, you model dishonesty and fear. The former encourages risk-taking, the latter discourages it.

For example, suppose a mother wants her young son's help in clearing the table after dinner. She can assertively ask for the help by saying something along these lines:

- "I want you to clear your place at the table when you've finished eating."
- "It's important to me that you help out by clearing your place at the table."
- "I need your help cleaning up; please clear your place at the table."

All three are assertive statements. In each, the mother makes her wants and expectations clear. More important, she assumes responsibility for her desires. Such phrases as "I want you to," "It's important to me," and "I need" all convey the message that it's normal and desirable to take responsibility for one's feelings and wants.

Here are a few manipulative messages that might be conveyed under the same circumstances:

- "Good little boys clear their place at the table when they're through eating."
- "If you loved me, you'd clear your place at the table."
- "You've really got to think of somebody other than yourself sometimes. Have a little consideration and clear your place at the table!"

In all three, the mother never clearly states that it's she who wants the youngster's help. Instead, she either labels the child and belittles him (unless the child clears his place, he is not a "good little boy"), or speaks as though she were voicing eternal truths rather than simply expressing her wants. Unlike the assertive statements, these suggest that it's unacceptable to openly express your wants, feelings, and needs.

Assertive Praise and Criticism

The assertive exercise of authority is one of the most powerful tools by which parents can encourage the self-acceptance at the heart of risk-taking. Assertively administered praise and criticism are a close second.

Properly given, praise and criticism can instill confidence and provide encouragement. Take the case of the toddler who wants to undress himself for the evening bath. He struggles for a few minutes to remove a pullover shirt. When the task is completed, his face beams with pride. The eyes that say, "I did it!" are asking for someone to recognize the accomplishment. Such comments as "You're wonderful!" or "You're terrific!" are nonconstructive. They're directed at the personality of the child rather than the accomplishment, thereby placing him in the position of having to live up to the label that's been applied. (It's not easy to be "wonderful" and "terrific" all the time.)

More useful and constructive praise centers on the accomplishment itself, not the personality of the youngster: "You sure got that shirt off!" "That was hard, but you did it!" Such comments focus on the deed and praise the child for what he's done, not for who he is. This distinction is essential to the development of a constructive attitude toward risk-taking.

Suppose the child is unable to remove the pullover. He is growing increasingly frustrated, and would certainly welcome help. Several responses are available to the parent at that point. They are listed in reverse order — the least desirable first.

- *"See, Bobby! I told you you couldn't do it. You're so obstinate sometimes!"* This is totally nonconstructive. It belittles the child and his efforts, labels him incapable and obstinate.

- *"See, Bobby! I told you you couldn't do it. Come here, let me do it for you!"* This is almost totally nonconstructive. While the parent does offer help, that help is phrased ("let me do it for you!") in a way that demeans the child. The help is paid for by admitting one's incapacity. The spunky child senses this and refuses the offer. But if the child isn't spunky, or if the youngster is genuinely incapable of performing the task, he gives in, and pays a large price for a little favor.

- *"Looks like you're having some trouble taking off that shirt. Can I help?"* This is the best of the three possible responses. It does not stigmatize or belittle the child. It consists only of a nonevaluative statement: the child appears to be in need of help. The parent's comment is a neutral observation, and is coupled with an offer of assistance. No price is asked in the form of diminished self-esteem. This is the kind of comment that simply places the parent where he or she belongs — behind the child, ready to back him up and provide help if asked. The comment further implies that the parent is willing to help the child, not do the task for him. Another time, perhaps tomorrow night, the child will be ready to take his shirt off by himself.

Other behaviors require a stronger response. Those that threaten the safety or comfort of the youngster or people around him need to be strongly discouraged. Although the big brother might be angry with his little sister, he simply cannot hurt her. The sensitive parent acknowledges the boy's feeling, and may even be willing to grant in fantasy what the youngster wants; but the adult makes a clear distinction between reality and fantasy, and forbids any violence. For instance, the parent might say, "I know you're angry with your sister; you may even wish you could punch her, but I won't let you. Let's talk." Such a response indicates acceptance of and respect for the child's feelings, while placing clear limitations on his behavior.

Most often, criticism is best offered in a form that describes the objectionable behavior and the feelings it engenders. The following formula, derived from the work of psychologist Thomas Gordon, provides useful guidance:

- *Step 1:* Describe the behavior (for example, "When you have a snack and don't clean up after yourself...").

- *Step 2:* Describe your feelings ("I get upset...").

- *Step 3:* Explain why the problematic behavior engenders that response ("...because I try hard to keep the house neat and I need your help to do it.").

This formula doesn't need to be followed slavishly. For example, depending on the circumstances, you might be able to leave out Step 3. The order in which you follow the steps can also vary. In the example given, it would be okay to say, "I get upset when you have a snack and don't clean up after yourself, because I try hard to keep the house neat and I need your help to do it." Here, Steps 1 and 2 are reversed, but the same point is made and nothing is lost in the message.

Negotiation

How you negotiate disagreements makes a difference in your youngster's attitudes toward risk. If you're upset with another person, do you tell her, or do you fume and complain to others? If you're dissatisfied with a purchase (food you're served in a restaurant, the paint job you've just had done, and so on), do you make your dissatisfaction known and insist that matters be set right, or do you sulk or displace your anger, directing it at others who are not to blame?

Suppose you do elect to confront someone under one of the circumstances proposed. If you model careful preparation, discipline, persistence, and firmness, these are the qualities your children will come to expect of themselves. They learn more by what you do than by what you say.

Expression of Feelings

How you express feelings also makes a big difference in your children's attitudes toward risk. Can you talk about your feelings openly? Do you distinguish between feeling a certain way and acting on that feeling? To the extent that you manage your feelings constructively, your children will learn to do the same.

The way you respond to your child's feelings is important, too. Listening for feelings and acknowledging them in a nonjudgmental way can do a great deal to promote your youngster's self-awareness and respect for feelings. Both are fundamental to risking.

Children usually say exactly how they feel. Only after they learn that certain feelings are "bad" do they begin burying them. For example, when you say to a child who has expressed hatred for someone or something, "It's not nice to hate," you've invalidated his feeling. It's better to accept the youngster's feeling and draw him out, while making clear the difference between feeling and acting on that feeling.

Helping Youngsters Define Themselves

Self-definition is a process we all must go through. It occurs in four stages, which I call *attribution, negative self-definition* (or *attribution rejection*), *external identity,* and *affirmation.* By helping your youngster negotiate these stages, you facilitate the development of risk-taking skills.

The attribution stage is that period in life when youngsters accept unquestioningly the characteristics others say they have. Infants and small children lack self-awareness and so accept without hesitation the characteristics attributed to them by others — much as a glass of water takes on the hue of vegetable coloring that's added to it. The youngster, having no frame of reference by which to judge what's been said, observes, "Mother says I'm lazy (or smart, or considerate), so I guess I am."

It's clear that negative attributions can be harmful: the child who is called "lazy" or told that she'll "never amount to anything" is likely to believe it. Less easy to see is that positive attributions can be harmful as well. Such labels as "considerate" and "intelligent" create expectations, as I said earlier, and can place pressure on a child.

Parents need to be particularly sensitive to labeling their youngsters. In praising and criticizing, it's always better to focus on behavior rather than personal traits.

During the negative self-definition stage, children shed the attributions given them by others. They become aware that their feelings and desires don't necessarily jibe with what they've been told about themselves. "No, I'm not always thoughtful," the youngster may say defiantly. This period is usually seen by others as a destructive, rebellious one. For better or worse, it is, for most people, inescapable. They must be able to say, "This is not me!" before they can say, "This is me!"

Parents need to accept this stage of growth and permit children an opportunity to experiment in the course of defining themselves. The risks they take at this time may seem entirely negative and to lack any redeeming value, but are crucial to the child's development.

During the external identity stage, youngsters are likely to adopt a dogma or model to serve as a temporary basis for self-definition. They may dress and act like an idealized hero — an athlete or a comic book character, for example — or commit themselves to a bizarre belief system.

Parents need to know that these models serve as temporary crutches, supporting young people until they have developed a strong enough sense of self to be able to stand alone. The best way to ensure that youngsters are able to let go of these crutches is to accept them as a temporary necessity. They almost certainly will not be a permanent part of your youngster's life.

The affirmation stage is that period when individuals turn inward, grow beyond rebellion, and affirm their past. They recognize that the beliefs they've espoused, the causes they've championed, the blunders they've made were all necessary prerequisites

Further Reading

Gardner, J. (1965) *Self-Renewal*. New York: Harper/Colophon Books.

Gordon, T. (1977) *Leader Effectiveness Training*. New York: Wyden Books.

Iacocca, L. (1984) *Iacocca: An Autobiography*. New York: Bantam Books.

Townsend, R. (1970) *Up the Organization*. New York: Alfred A. Knopf.

10

The Personal Consequences
of Risk

Joy accompanies the self-affirmation of our
essential being....
— Paul Tillich, *The Courage To Be*

Whether your risks are practical or psychological, they will have personal and interpersonal dimensions; you'll almost certainly change as a result of becoming a risk-taker. Your relationships with others will change as well.

Part One: Personal Changes

There are many personal changes that occur when you've learned to risk. The most important include:

- Increased autonomy
- Heightened self-esteem
- A more positive attitude toward life
- An increased sense of personal power

Each of these changes is discussed below.

Increased Autonomy

Significant risks almost always involve breaking away from the secure and the familiar, overcoming infantile dependencies, and confronting life, perhaps for the first time, on your own two feet. It can be said that the chief personal consequence of risking is increased autonomy. When you've begun to risk successfully, you are bound to emerge as an active, creative force in molding your own destiny, seizing control of your life, and assuming responsibility for it.

Psychological risk-takers confront the challenge of being human. Rather than shrinking back in trepidation, they move forward.

Fear and hesitation are a legitimate part of this process. With each such risk, you develop your capacities, becoming more autonomous, more truly yourself.

This moving forward is not an event that's fixed in time; it's not like throwing a switch. Rather, it is a process, a gradual movement forward over many years. Along the way, there are pauses, lapses, slowdowns, regressions. And there is no guarantee that the process, once begun, will end successfully. The struggle for fulfillment is an endless one. Goethe said it very well: "He only earns his freedom and existence who daily conquers them anew."

There is perhaps some consolation in the fact that once you've started on the path toward autonomy, each positive choice makes the next one easier. With each courageous act, you become more courageous. With each self-disclosure risk, for example, self-disclosure becomes more natural and familiar.

Heightened Self-Esteem

An important consequence of taking risks successfully is an increase in your self-esteem. Each time you complete a difficult task or meet a risky and self-expanding challenge, your self-esteem grows. You begin to see yourself as resourceful, capable, and resilient. No matter what you're confronted with in the future, you know that you have the potential to emerge from any encounter a wiser, stronger person.

Your heightened self-esteem may result in major external changes. You may change your job, get married or divorced, leave your family of origin, or relocate to another part of the country.

More likely, you'll make less radical changes. Many risk-takers report that while they do not completely alter their lifestyles, they do find themselves redefining their relationships, behaving more assertively, becoming less willing to tolerate people in their lives who serve as unwanted emotional ballast. Because your self-esteem does not depend on others thinking well of you, you are free to select as friends those people with whom you can be completely yourself. You form relationships not out of weakness, but from a position of strength, with an openness to growing and learning with heartfelt love and regard.

A More Positive Attitude Toward Life

When you learn to risk, you experience a general upturn in optimism and good feelings, an openness to life and experience, and delight in the present moment.

Not surprisingly, your attitude is one of curiosity and wonder. You refuse to cope with the world in fixed ways, but always manage to be flexible and open to new ideas. You don't try to deny change, or to prevent it. Instead, you recognize that change is the essence of life. Your continuing task is to cope with the fluid psychological moment. Moreover, because you're open to change and growth, you find yourself increasingly able to cope. With each creative adjustment, your capacity to adjust creatively grows stronger. With each expansion of the self, you are better able to expand yourself once again.

An Increased Sense of Your Personal Power

As a risk-taker, you develop a new respect for your power. You recognize that as long as you remain open to experience, there is no end to your ability to learn and grow. The key to growth is simply the willingness to risk, to let go, to venture.

Accompanying success as a risk-taker is a feeling of liberation from an obsessive need for others, of knowing that you can fend for yourself in the world. You realize that you need never shy away from any reasonable challenge. You have resilience and adaptability, and skills that will help you prepare for every risk you undertake.

Part Two: Interpersonal Changes

An openness to risk tends to improve your personal relationships as you become more accepting of others because you're less dependent on them, and less inclined to judge or control them. Your openness makes you more sensitive to other people, and more willing to help them in meaningful ways. Again, you'll tend to redefine important relationships along healthier lines, and to end relationships with people who cannot or will not maintain psychologically clean, unencumbered ties.

Acceptance of Others

A feeling of peace often pervades the risk-taker's relationships with others. That doesn't mean that you'll always be pleased with others, or invulnerable to hurt or rejection. But you probably are more able than most to accept other people for who they are, rather than trying to make them fit your image of who you want them to be. Because you're more satisfied with yourself, you feel less pressure to fulfill your needs through others; and, consequently, you're better able to be a loving partner, parent, or friend.

Sensitivity and Your Ability to Help Others

Risk-takers are able to respond meaningfully to the needs and problems of others — to serve as a friend, resource, and supporter in times of need. Two things make this possible. The first is increased sensitivity. When you're freed of the need to prove yourself, to rationalize your failures away, to win approval, and so on, it becomes possible to focus on others, to become attuned to their needs.

Finally, your own feeling of fulfillment makes it easy to take the time to get to know others as they really are, and to respond cheerfully to their needs. There are few people better able to help others than those who are content with themselves. This is what accounts for people like Mother Theresa.

Redefinition of Relationships

Sweeping personal changes almost always cause you to take stock of your relationships. You may find that a specific relationship is exactly where it should be and that it requires no changes. For example, a relationship that's characterized by mutual acceptance, trust, open communication, and the absence of manipulation is fine just the way it is.

Other relationships may fall short of your ideal. You have several options. You can accept these faulty relationships as they are, realizing that there is little you can do to change them. This occurred when one middle-aged man realized that his elderly mother was very unlikely to change. Though she was manipulative and their relationship was flawed in many ways, he cherished her nonetheless. Despite her faults and the peculiarities of the relationship, he elected to leave things as they were.

If the relationship stands the chance of being improved, and if you value it sufficiently, you may elect to try to make it better. There are no guarantees that you'll succeed. (The effort is itself a risk!) Nor can you be at all certain that the other person involved will be willing to change.

But you can try. If change is to occur at all, it can't be done by telling the other person how he or she should behave. Fault-finding won't work either, or moralizing, or being what one acquaintance of mine calls a "psycho-pest." Any change in a relationship can only be brought about by changing yourself. For example, by communicating openly and assertively, and by making your own choices and assuming responsibility for them within the context of the relationship, you will be doing what you can to make the change possible. The rest is up to the other person.

If earnest efforts to improve a relationship still fail, sometimes the tough choice of ending it is all that's left. Ending a friendship may mean never seeing that person again. Or it may mean maintaining a distant enough tie to allow you to be emotionally uninvolved.

You may find that the other person takes the initiative in terminating your relationship. Sometimes changes you undergo can be intolerable to the people in your life. They may be used to things being the way they've always been; this can be the case even if things have always been bad. Often people have co-dependent relationships, so that one partner's frailty is the other partner's livelihood: the alcoholic who stops drinking, the overweight partner who suddenly gets slim, the perennial loser who begins to find purpose and discipline — all can be terribly threatening to the balance of an unbalanced relationship. You might find that the "reward" for all your effort to grow and change is that your loved ones fight you at every step of the way, or even abandon you.

If you find yourself in such a situation, try to surround yourself with other people who support your self-improvement.

There can certainly be an unanticipated downside to risk-taking. But even outwardly devastating losses can harbor long-term psychological gains. Use this book, and any other resources you can find, to help you gauge the ups and downs of every risk, and to keep *your goals in the forefront of your consciousness and clearly defined.*

A Final Word

All growth demands that you overcome your hunger for security. Therefore every self-expanding choice is experienced as risky. If you're a person who's comfortable taking risks, the information you've read in this book has probably reinforced thoughts and strategies already familiar to you. We hope that the book has provided you with some fresh perspectives on the matter of risk and growth.

If you've been stymied by guilt, fear, or any of the other impediments to risk-taking, we hope that this book has provided you both useful tools and inspiration. Please be assured that you can begin taking meaningful risks at any point in your life, whether you're sixteen or sixty. We hope you'll use our ideas wisely and benefit from them.

Further Reading

May, R. (1967) *Man's Search for Himself*. New York: Signet Books.
Tillich, P. (1952) *The Courage To Be*. New Haven, Connecticut: Yale University Press.